# SpringerBriefs in Education

We are delighted to announce SpringerBriefs in Education, an innovative product type that combines elements of both journals and books. Briefs present concise summaries of cutting-edge research and practical applications in education. Featuring compact volumes of 50 to 125 pages, the SpringerBriefs in Education allow authors to present their ideas and readers to absorb them with a minimal time investment. Briefs are published as part of Springer's eBook Collection. In addition, Briefs are available for individual print and electronic purchase.

SpringerBriefs in Education cover a broad range of educational fields such as: Science Education, Higher Education, Educational Psychology, Assessment & Evaluation, Language Education, Mathematics Education, Educational Technology, Medical Education and Educational Policy.

SpringerBriefs typically offer an outlet for:

- An introduction to a (sub)field in education summarizing and giving an overview of theories, issues, core concepts and/or key literature in a particular field
- A timely report of state-of-the art analytical techniques and instruments in the field of educational research
- A presentation of core educational concepts
- An overview of a testing and evaluation method
- A snapshot of a hot or emerging topic or policy change
- An in-depth case study
- A literature review
- A report/review study of a survey
- An elaborated thesis

Both solicited and unsolicited manuscripts are considered for publication in the SpringerBriefs in Education series. Potential authors are warmly invited to complete and submit the Briefs Author Proposal form. All projects will be submitted to editorial review by editorial advisors.

SpringerBriefs are characterized by expedited production schedules with the aim for publication 8 to 12 weeks after acceptance and fast, global electronic dissemination through our online platform SpringerLink. The standard concise author contracts guarantee that:

- an individual ISBN is assigned to each manuscript
- each manuscript is copyrighted in the name of the author
- the author retains the right to post the pre-publication version on his/her website or that of his/her institution

Jinghe Han

# English Medium Instruction as a Local Practice

Language, culture and pedagogy

Jinghe Han
School of Education, Centre for Educational Research
Western Sydney University
Penrith, NSW, Australia

This work was supported by Western Sydney University

ISSN 2211-1921                ISSN 2211-193X   (electronic)
SpringerBriefs in Education
ISBN 978-3-031-19903-5        ISBN 978-3-031-19904-2   (eBook)
https://doi.org/10.1007/978-3-031-19904-2

© The Author(s) 2023. This book is an open access publication.

**Open Access** This book is licensed under the terms of the Creative Commons Attribution 4.0 International License (http://creativecommons.org/licenses/by/4.0/), which permits use, sharing, adaptation, distribution and reproduction in any medium or format, as long as you give appropriate credit to the original author(s) and the source, provide a link to the Creative Commons license and indicate if changes were made.

The images or other third party material in this book are included in the book's Creative Commons license, unless indicated otherwise in a credit line to the material. If material is not included in the book's Creative Commons license and your intended use is not permitted by statutory regulation or exceeds the permitted use, you will need to obtain permission directly from the copyright holder.

The use of general descriptive names, registered names, trademarks, service marks, etc. in this publication does not imply, even in the absence of a specific statement, that such names are exempt from the relevant protective laws and regulations and therefore free for general use.

The publisher, the authors, and the editors are safe to assume that the advice and information in this book are believed to be true and accurate at the date of publication. Neither the publisher nor the authors or the editors give a warranty, expressed or implied, with respect to the material contained herein or for any errors or omissions that may have been made. The publisher remains neutral with regard to jurisdictional claims in published maps and institutional affiliations.

This Springer imprint is published by the registered company Springer Nature Switzerland AG
The registered company address is: Gewerbestrasse 11, 6330 Cham, Switzerland

# Acknowledgments

My thanks and appreciation go to Springer and the book series editor Emeritus Professor Chris Davison and Professor Xuesong (Andy) Gao for providing a platform for this research to reach an international audience.

I would like to acknowledge Professor Michele Simons, Dean of the School of Education, for her continuous support during the writing of this book.

The evidence for this book was collected from EMI colleagues at Huaqiao University. I appreciate their generosity in terms of sharing ideas and accepting the invitation to allow me to be present in their class and observe their teaching.

I particularly would like to express my sincere thanks to my dear colleague and friend Lin Brown for her continued support through the many discussions on the intentions of this book. On many occasions, her positivity provided inspiration as the writing progressed through its many phases and competing demands.

Jinghe Han
Penrith
September 2022

# Contents

**1 English Medium Instruction: Expanding Notions of English Hegemony and Colonization** .................... 1
  1.1 Introduction ................................................. 1
  1.2 Research into English Medium Instruction ................... 3
  1.3 The Context of EMI Teaching and Research in China .......... 5
  1.4 The Research Supporting This Book ........................... 7
    1.4.1 Data Collection ..................................... 8
  1.5 Book Structure ............................................ 8
  References .................................................... 10

**2 Conceptualization of English Medium Instruction** ............... 17
  2.1 Introduction ............................................... 17
  2.2 Conceptualizing 'ENGLISH' in EMI ........................... 18
    2.2.1 Should Native English Be the Norm for EMI Lecturers? ............................... 19
    2.2.2 Is It 'English' or 'Englishes' in EMI? ............... 19
    2.2.3 Translanguaging – The Nature of EMI Teaching ......... 20
  2.3 The 'MEDIUM' in EMI ........................................ 21
    2.3.1 Impacts of Medium on Language Use .................. 23
    2.3.2 Medium in Relation to Mode, Field, Tenor and Context ........................................ 23
  2.4 The 'INSTRUCTION' in EMI .................................. 24
  2.5 Conclusion ................................................ 26
  References .................................................... 27

**3 Chinese Lecturers' Pedagogical Position and Instructional Practice in EMI Teaching** ..................................... 31
  3.1 Introduction ............................................... 31
  3.2 Pedagogy and Approaches to Instruction ..................... 33

|   |   |   |   |
|---|---|---|---|
|   | 3.3 | Literature of Pedagogical Positioning and Instructional Practice in China . . . . . . . . . . . . . . . . . . . . . . . . . . . . . . . . . . . . . . . | 34 |
|   |   | 3.3.1 The EMI Lecturers' Perception of Teaching and Learning . . . . . . . . . . . . . . . . . . . . . . . . . . . . . . . . . . . . . | 35 |
|   |   | 3.3.2 EMI Lecturers' Additional Comments. . . . . . . . . . . . . . . . . . | 38 |
|   |   | 3.3.3 The Design Features of EMI Lecturers' Instruction . . . . . . | 39 |
|   |   | 3.3.4 Topic-Based Versus Problem-Centered Instruction . . . . . . . | 39 |
|   |   | 3.3.5 Instruction Linking Prior and New Knowledge. . . . . . . . . . | 41 |
|   |   | 3.3.6 Teacher Talk and Knowledge Demonstration/Explanation by the Lecturer . . . . . . . . . . . . . | 42 |
|   |   | 3.3.7 New Knowledge Application and Integration by the Students in the Real World . . . . . . . . . . . . . . . . . . . . | 43 |
|   | 3.4 | The Chinese Lecturers' Pedagogical and Instructional Choice – Cultural or Rational? . . . . . . . . . . . . . . . . . . . . . . . . . . . . . | 45 |
|   | 3.5 | Lecturers' Discipline Knowledge and Teaching . . . . . . . . . . . . . . . | 45 |
|   | 3.6 | Learners–Passive in Behavior but Active in Thinking. . . . . . . . . . . | 46 |
|   | 3.7 | Conclusion . . . . . . . . . . . . . . . . . . . . . . . . . . . . . . . . . . . . . . . . . . . . . . | 47 |
|   | References. . . . . . . . . . . . . . . . . . . . . . . . . . . . . . . . . . . . . . . . . . . . . . . . . . . . | | 47 |
| 4 | **Chinese EMI Lecturers' Engagement Strategies**. . . . . . . . . . . . . . . . . . | | 51 |
|   | 4.1 | Introduction – Does the Choice of Pedagogy and Instruction Impact Engagement?. . . . . . . . . . . . . . . . . . . . . . . . . | 51 |
|   | 4.2 | Engagement as a Concept . . . . . . . . . . . . . . . . . . . . . . . . . . . . . . . . . | 53 |
|   | 4.3 | Data – EMI Teaching and Engagement . . . . . . . . . . . . . . . . . . . . . . | 55 |
|   |   | 4.3.1 Cognitive Strategies – Chinese EMI Lecturers' Strength. . . . . . . . . . . . . . . . . . . . . . . . . . . . . . . . . . | 55 |
|   |   | 4.3.2 Emotional Engagement – Distancing Students for Complex Reasons. . . . . . . . . . . . . . . . . . . . . . . . . . . . . . | 57 |
|   |   | 4.3.3 Limited Behavioral and Managerial Engagement . . . . . . . . | 60 |
|   | 4.4 | Linguistic Features in Engagement Activities . . . . . . . . . . . . . . . . . | 61 |
|   | 4.5 | Discussion – Engagement, Language and Tenor? . . . . . . . . . . . . . . | 62 |
|   | 4.6 | Conclusion . . . . . . . . . . . . . . . . . . . . . . . . . . . . . . . . . . . . . . . . . . . . . . | 63 |
|   | References. . . . . . . . . . . . . . . . . . . . . . . . . . . . . . . . . . . . . . . . . . . . . . . . . . . . | | 64 |
| 5 | **Cross-Linguistic Influence: Bilingual EMI Lecturers' English and Chinese Entwined** . . . . . . . . . . . . . . . . . . . . . . . . . . . . . . | | 67 |
|   | 5.1 | Introduction . . . . . . . . . . . . . . . . . . . . . . . . . . . . . . . . . . . . . . . . . . . . . | 67 |
|   | 5.2 | Cross-Linguistic Influence. . . . . . . . . . . . . . . . . . . . . . . . . . . . . . . . . | 69 |
|   |   | 5.2.1 Negative vs Positive or Explicit vs Implicit Transfer . . . . . | 69 |
|   | 5.3 | L1-Influenced English Identified in the EMI Lecturers' Teaching . . . . . . . . . . . . . . . . . . . . . . . . . . . . . . . . . . . . . . | 70 |
|   |   | 5.3.1 Phonological Influence – Consonants, Vowels and Consonant-Vowel Complex. . . . . . . . . . . . . . . . . . . . . . | 71 |
|   |   | 5.3.2 L1 Influence on the Syntactic Structure of English . . . . . . . | 72 |

|  |  | 5.3.3 | EMI Lecturers' Semantic Transfer. | 74 |
|---|---|---|---|---|
|  |  | 5.3.4 | EMI Lecturers' Conceptual Transfer | 75 |
|  |  | 5.3.5 | Reverse Transfer | 77 |
|  | 5.4 | Discussion | | 78 |
|  |  | 5.4.1 | Nativeness – An Aspiration for EMI Lecturers | 78 |
|  | 5.5 | Conclusion | | 80 |
|  | References | | | 80 |
| 6 | **Pragmatic Transfer: Reflecting on the Use of EMI Lecturers' Pragmatic Markers** | | | 83 |
|  | 6.1 | Introduction | | 83 |
|  | 6.2 | Research into Bilinguals' Pragmatic Transfer and Pragmatic Markers | | 84 |
|  | 6.3 | Functional Categorization of Pragmatic Markers | | 86 |
|  | 6.4 | Pragmatic Strategies in the Chinese Lecturers' EMI Classes | | 88 |
|  |  | 6.4.1 | Conceptual Cognitive Markers | 89 |
|  |  | 6.4.2 | Interpersonal Markers | 89 |
|  |  | 6.4.3 | Organizational Markers – Causation, Collection and Continuity, Description, Comparison and Problem/Solution | 90 |
|  |  | 6.4.4 | Pragmatic Markers in EMI and CMI | 92 |
|  | 6.5 | Discussion – The Influential Factors to the Chinese Lecturers' Pragmatic Strategies | | 92 |
|  |  | 6.5.1 | Pedagogical Influence | 93 |
|  |  | 6.5.2 | Contextual Influence | 94 |
|  |  | 6.5.3 | Influence from Subject Matter | 94 |
|  |  | 6.5.4 | Language Influence | 94 |
|  | 6.6 | Conclusion | | 95 |
|  | References | | | 95 |
| 7 | **When Structuralism and Post-structuralism Collide: EMI Lecturers' Monolingual Ideology and Translanguaging Practice.** | | | 99 |
|  | 7.1 | Introduction | | 99 |
|  | 7.2 | A Post-structuralist Theorization of Translanguaging | | 101 |
|  |  | 7.2.1 | Going 'Between' and 'Beyond' Languages. | 101 |
|  |  | 7.2.2 | Translanguaging as a Process | 102 |
|  |  | 7.2.3 | Multilingual Ideology of Translanguaging | 103 |
|  |  | 7.2.4 | Translanguaging as Pedagogical Practice | 103 |
|  |  | 7.2.5 | Translanguaging Identity | 104 |
|  | 7.3 | Chinese EMI Lecturers' Language Ideology vs Translanguaging Practice | | 105 |
|  |  | 7.3.1 | EMI Lecturers' Monolingual vs Bi/Multilingual Ideology | 105 |
|  |  | 7.3.2 | EMI Lecturers' Language Identity. | 106 |

|  |  | 7.3.3 | Translanguaging Practice as the Norm in EMI Teaching.............................. | 108 |
|---|---|---|---|---|
|  |  | 7.3.4 | Translanguaging for Emotional Connection with Students ................................. | 110 |
|  | 7.4 | Discussion ............................................... | | 111 |
|  | 7.5 | Conclusion............................................... | | 112 |
|  | References.................................................... | | | 112 |
| 8 | **The Research on English Medium Instruction and a Proposed Constructivist EMI Teaching Framework**......... | | | **117** |
|  | 8.1 | The Research ............................................ | | 117 |
|  | 8.2 | Summary of the Research ................................ | | 119 |
|  | 8.3 | A Proposed Constructivist EMI Teaching Framework .......... | | 122 |
|  | 8.4 | A Brief Epilogue ........................................ | | 125 |
|  | References.................................................... | | | 126 |

# About the Author

**Jinghe Han** (PhD) is Professor of Language Education at the Centre for Educational Research in the School of Education, Western Sydney University. Her research areas include bilingual language teacher education, translanguaging, and English as a medium of instruction. She is author of the books *Theorising Culture – A Chinese Perspective* and *Post-lingual Pedagogy: Hanzi Method*. Jinghe is also actively researching the pedagogy of HDR teaching. She is co-author of the book *Pedagogies for Internationalising Research Education* and has successfully supervised 50 HDR students to completion in the past 10 years. Email: j.han@westernsydney.edu.au

# List of Figures

Fig. 2.1   Mapping the 'medium' in EMI ........................................................ 22
Fig. 3.1   Teacher talk and knowledge demonstration ..................................... 43
Fig. 3.2   Student time in knowledge application into the real-world .............. 44

# List of Tables

| | | |
|---|---|---|
| Table 1.1 | Summary of data collection protocol | 8 |
| Table 3.1 | EMI lecturers' pedagogical standing (Survey data) | 36 |
| Table 3.2 | Observation of EMI lecturers' instruction | 40 |
| Table 4.1 | Cognitive strategies demonstrated by EMI lecturers | 56 |
| Table 4.2 | Instructional signs | 61 |
| Table 4.3 | Divisiveness in the use of pronouns | 62 |
| Table 5.1 | Phonological transfer | 72 |
| Table 5.2 | Observed explicit syntactic transfer | 73 |
| Table 5.3 | Examples of semantic transfer | 74 |
| Table 5.4 | Examples of reverse transfer | 77 |
| Table 6.1 | Functional categorization of pragmatic markers | 88 |
| Table 6.2 | Cognitive markers | 89 |
| Table 6.3 | Interpersonal markers | 90 |
| Table 6.4 | EMI lecturers' use of organizational PMs | 91 |
| Table 7.1 | EMI lecturers' monolingual vs bi/multilingual views of their instructional languages | 106 |
| Table 7.2 | EMI lecturers' language identity | 107 |
| Table 7.3 | Translanguaging as scaffolds | 108 |
| Table 7.4 | Translanguaging and cognitive processing | 109 |
| Table 7.5 | Translanguaging as a mean of interpersonal connection | 110 |
| Table 8.1 | Constructivist EMI teaching framework | 123 |

# Chapter 1
# English Medium Instruction: Expanding Notions of English Hegemony and Colonization

**Abstract** This Chapter provides the background to the EMI research undertaken which has provided the evidence base for this book. It acknowledges internationalization of higher education within the current neoliberal global economy, and the swift move in the countries of the Expanding Circle towards EMI delivery as a strategy to expand academics' and universities' global agendas. This Chapter points to the theoretical and methodological limitations in current EMI research as convenient and unsystematic. Consequently, the knowledge generation to inform EMI teaching is limited. It concludes with an outline of the structure of the book highlighting the key foci for each Chapter.

**Keywords** English Medium Instruction · Internationalization of higher education · English hegemony and colonization · Pedagogy for EMI teaching

## 1.1 Introduction

Teaching through English [as the] Medium of Instruction (EMI) has arisen in unison with the emergent internationalization of education within the current global economy. It continues to trend upwards and has secured a strong foothold in higher education systems where English is not the vernacular. It has been implemented at many universities worldwide, particularly in those countries described by Kachru (1985) as being in the Outer or Expanding Circles, in terms of the spread of English across the globe. The motives, or a country's strategic agenda, for establishing EMI programs are dynamic but mostly driven by economic and political forces as universities respond to increasing competition over global resources (Wilkinson, 2012, p. 11) and in the context where global careers operate almost completely in English. The bourgeoning of EMI teaching in European and Asian higher education systems, that is, countries in the Expanding Circle where English is a foreign language, has been observed as escalating EMI's position as a new 'colonial frontier' (Doiz et al., 2012 p. xvii). As such, EMI is continually marketed and uncritically promoted and accepted by policy makers in these regions in spite of contestations, for example, that educators and learners respond more creatively and critically when thinking in their first language (Phillipson, 2017).

EMI programs are touted as an innovation of content and language integrated teaching (Brüning & Purrmann, 2014; Coyle et al., 2010). Europe's EMI teaching is currently presented as a best-practice scenario although evidence of consistent achievement across countries is lacking. It has been described as a strategic move to internationalize the curriculum and accreditation in the European Union's (EU) higher education (Costa & Coleman, 2013; Macaro & Akincioglu, 2018; Werther et al., 2014). In Europe, EMI teaching dates back to the 1990's as evidenced in the Bologna Declaration (1999), which proposed objectives for tertiary education reform. The implementation of EMI programs largely reflects a country's economic and educational status, depending on whether it has sufficient resources to attract overseas students into its higher education space. In this regard, Western and Northern Europe countries have demonstrated advantages (De Wit et al., 2015).

For various reasons, some Asian countries and regions are moving swiftly toward EMI delivery in their higher education sectors. The Chinese Ministry of Education (MOE) prioritized EMI teaching into higher education policy as a direct implementation of the country's strategic plan: to develop First Class World Universities, First Class Academic Discipline Development, and to achieve the gold standard destination for international students (Ren, 2016). In Taiwan, to address declining enrolments in its higher education sector, EMI teaching has been introduced and promoted as a 'national movement' – a concerted effort to attract international students (Chen & Tsai, 2012, p. 195; Huang & Singh, 2014). Korea, Vietnam and other East and Southeast Asian countries are expanding their international reach increasing the demand for a skilled labor force with high English proficiency in business processes and content (Kim et al., 2017a, b; Lee & Lee, 2018; MOET, 2008). This drives their higher education sectors to improve the quality of graduates through EMI programs.

EMI is widely accepted as using English to teach academic subjects in an English as a foreign language context (Dearden, 2014). It seems irrelevant to Inner Circle countries where English is the first language (Kachru, 1985). Rather, it arises as serious 'business' for those countries in the Expanding and Outer Circles reflecting their commitment to a neoliberal economy. EMI can therefore be considered a sign of the deepening entrenchment of English colonization around the world. Countries such as the U.S.A., the U.K., Australia, Canada and New Zealand in the Inner Circle continuingly enjoy the profit and convenience of having English as the/a national language and the hegemonic position this enables. The hegemonic position of English also benefits countries such as Singapore, India and Malaysia, in the Outer Circle. The long history of English colonization enabled these former colonies to provide education through EMI across all sectors (Phillipson, 2017). Their position in the global marketplace is therefore more favourable in attracting international students, compared to those in the Expanding Circle in terms of visibility, the competition for talented students, and graduate employability world-wide.

For academics and students in Northern Europe, EMI teaching has the advantage of linking to their first language (L1), in that there is a genetic link (Ersheidat & Tahir, 2020) with both language systems being alphabetic. In contrast, most Asian languages (Expanding Circle countries) are genetically and linguistically distant from English (Arabaski & Wojtaszek, 2015) thus teaching through EMI for academic staff in this context can be very challenging. Most have no experience of EMI in their own education and rarely have received upskilling through professional learning to teach subject knowledge through EMI (Phan, 2022). Nevertheless, proponents of neoliberalism, view English Medium Instruction as a strategy to expand academics' and universities' repertoires (Dimova et al. 2015) and will aid the "linguistic capital accumulation" of learners (Phillipson, 2017, p. 323). This view is countered by scholars such as Bunce et al. (2016), promoting overwhelming benefits to the scientific principles of 'mother-tongue' based multilingual education (Bunce et al., 2016). However, active neoliberal policies in some universities have largely contributed to the development of their EMI programs. For example some Scandinavian and East Asian universities offer additional remuneration and incentives such as overseas trips to academics who teach and publish in English (Phillipson, 2018; Quan et al., 2017; Rose et al., 2020).

## 1.2 Research into English Medium Instruction

Research on EMI teaching in the last 30 years has progressed across the field, yet a major focus continues to be problem identification. Consistently reported have been three main trends or problem areas: English language issues; pedagogical and professional learning issues; and stakeholders' opinions of EMI teaching in general. The propensity of this type of research suggests a saturation point has been reached and the need for a new vision is required – that of, problem solving (Macaro & Akincioglu, 2018).

The strand of research that focuses on general English usage tends to treat EMI as comparable to EFL or ESL (Björkman, 2016). At the level of the individual, English proficiency or lack thereof, is reported as the key challenge for EMI teaching (Ament & Pérez-Vidal, 2015; Basturkmen, 2018; Doiz & Lasagabaster, 2018; Jenkins, 2018; Jiang et al., 2019; Kumiko, 2018). Institutionally, universities were criticized as lacking suitable criteria and training when or after recruiting EMI lecturers and especially not implementing standardized English benchmark testing as a pre-requisite (Goodman et al., 2022; Lasagabaster, 2018). This is despite the contention that lecturers who were believed to have good oral English were assigned to teach in EMI programs (Dearden, 2014). In addition, EMI professional learning for academics was often facilitated by language experts from within Linguistics/Language Centers rather than drawing on the expertise of education faculties (Mancho-Barés & Arnó-Macià, 2017; Wilkinson & Zegers, 2008). Further the content of EMI training was identified as short courses based on 'general English proficiency', 'academic English', or 'English for teaching' (Mancho-Barés & Arnó-Macià 2017). At the individual level, when seeking professional development, EMI lecturers tended to also narrow their focus to English language proficiency. Studies have reported that English is the main concern of EMI lecturers who often criticized their own English as being non-colloquial and 'accented' and exemplifying poor communication skills (Dalton-Puffer, 2013; Gustafson, 2018; He & Chiang, 2016; Tsou & Kao, 2017). These concerns and/or efforts demonstrate a reductive approach to EMI from not only an institutional viewpoint but also from EMI professionals.

Along with English-focused research, earlier scholars promote an anti-neoliberal view and critique the intrinsic English hegemonic operation within EMI programs (de Cillia & Schweiger, 2001; Ljosland, 2014; Mortensen, 2014; Mühleisen, 2003; Phillipson, 2006). Since then Björkman (2016, p. 57) challenged the findings of these studies as being uncritical contending "they are more investigatory in general" rather than offering specific insight. To further Bjorkman's (2016) argument, consideration could be given to addressing how EMI lecturers' bilingual repertoires can be developed to strengthen their EMI teaching. More recently, research has reported the role of lecturers' L1 within their EMI teaching (Lin & Lo, 2017; Muguruza et al., 2020; Sah & Li, 2022; Tai & Li, 2021). This has somewhat broken the silences around actual translanguaging practices situated within "English" Medium of Instruction. It challenges the status quo's taken-for-granted choice of EMI teaching – designed to assert a monolingual set of priorities. This research has been noteworthy given the majority of EMI lecturers, if not all, are bilingual (or multilingual), and English is not insulated from their L1. In cognitive practice bilinguals or multilinguals naturally activate their repertoire of background language/s when using English (Gunnarsson et al., 2015, p. 16). English is the 'official' instructional language in EMI teaching, but EMI teachers' bi/multilingual reality implies that cross-linguistic transfer and translanguaging is a significant phenomenon in EMI classrooms. This is confirmed in the report by Rose et al. (2020, p. 14), who found, "in practice, students and teachers report multilingualism and bilingualism as normal practice in EMI classrooms".

Researchers have called for pedagogical training as a solution to the problem of improving the success of EMI teaching and learning (Ismailov et al., 2021; Macaro & Akincioglu, 2018), signalling that lecturers' pedagogy needs improvement. Literature reports that a number of universities offering EMI programs admitted they did not provide pedagogical training to EMI lecturers (Dearden, 2015; O'Dowd, 2018). As Alhassan (2021) reports, "…little research thus far seems to have focused on EMI subject teacher challenges and training needs". In addition, an international survey, completed by a number of universities globally found that pedagogy for EMI teaching was "far from being treated as an important issue" and there was not "sufficient attention to the training and accreditation of the teachers [or lecturers] engaged in EMI" (O'Dowd, 2018, p. 557). Under the related category of Content and Language Integrated Learning (CLIL), there are some published discussions on promoting a 'dual focus on language and content learning', leading to a belief that EMI or CLIL methodology can increase lecturers' awareness of how language may affect the construction of disciplinary understanding (Kampen et al., 2018; Mancho-Barés & Arnó-Macià, 2017). Others argue that lecturers should focus on content and tolerate some deviation from the standard usage of the teaching language (González

Ardeo, 2013; Wilson & Devereux, 2014). These propositions are articulating a way forward in the development of useful CLIL or EMI pedagogies.

Other studies report the provision of professional learning for EMI lecturers (Cots, 2012; O'Dowd, 2018; Shohamy, 2012). According to these reports, some training is often not needs-based but rather concessions to convenience. For example, Wächter and Maiworm (2014) reported a study with the single focus to improve EMI lecturers' English. Macaro, et al. (2018) conducted a systematic review of EMI teaching and concluded that professional learning often did not include any reflection or critique of existing EMI teaching pedagogies as a starting point to improve practice. For example, one EMI training program reported, involved participating lecturers presenting their teaching, supplemented by evaluation and feedback from peers. This training program was regarded as successful because the focus was for lecturers to reflect on their own teaching practice (Macaro & Akincioglu, 2018). No evidence was provided on how EMI lecturers could transform these reflections to inform the development of their EMI teaching repertoires. The review indicates that there is a notable absence of evidence-based training programs. Further there is little scientifically recorded observation-based classroom data to inform the EMI lecturers' professional development.

In addition to English proficiency, and pedagogical problems and professional learning challenges (Alhassen, 2021), there is a body of literature reporting research 'about' EMI from the perspective of stakeholders. This includes EMI lecturers' and/or students' perceptions and beliefs about EMI in teaching and learning (Dearden & Macaro, 2016; Kling, 2013; Kuteeva & Airey, 2014); lecturers and/or students' attitudes towards EMI programs (Arnó-Macià & Mancho-Barés, 2015; Dearden, 2014; Dearden & Macaro, 2016); universities' opinions on the usefulness of EMI training (O'Dowd, 2018); national, institutional and personal thoughts about EMI (Hu & Lei, 2014a, b) and students' expectations of learning through EMI classes (Kim, 2011). Whilst acknowledging investigations into beliefs, perceptions and attitudes associated with EMI contributes to a better understanding of the complexity of EMI teaching, for EMI research to move forward, retrospective participant accounts have their limitations. Chen et al. (2020) and Macaro et al. (2018) have argued that EMI research should assign attention to actual pedagogical practices in EMI classrooms by including participation by the researcher/s.

## 1.3 The Context of EMI Teaching and Research in China

In China, EMI has had a relatively short history commencing some two decades previous (Xu, 2021), followed by a series of policy initiatives (Rose et al., 2020). In 2001 the then Prime Minister Zhu Rongji proposed the implementation of EMI as a cross-curricula innovation to raise China's capability for knowledge exchange with the world (Chen & Yu, 2018). In 2010, the China State Council promulgated the *Outline of the National Medium and Long-term Education Reform and Development Plan* (2010–2020), proposing to draw on current international education ideologies and practices for China's educational reform and development. In response, EMI teaching as an important teaching mode was introduced (Gu et al., 2020). The Ministry of Education of China echoed this by affirming that EMI courses can enhance the international employability of local graduates, attract overseas students to study in China and improve the competitiveness of China's higher education globally (Hu & Lei, 2014a, b; Liu, 2020). In this context it was recommended that a university should have 5–10% of undergraduate courses taught in English (Hu & Lei, 2014a, b).

In 2015, the China State Council disseminated *the General Plan for Coordinating the Construction of World-Class Universities and First-Class Disciplines*, a program for the construction of 'double first-class' universities, aiming to reach international standards for first class universities and first-class disciplines (Rose et al., 2020). A recent report commissioned by the British Council in China in collaboration with the EMI Oxford Research Group (Rose et al., 2020, p. 5) referred to the ongoing "Double First Class" program stating its goal is to "…make China an international HE power by the middle of the 21$^{st}$ century". In the wake of these reforms constructing relevant courses to be taught via EMI was again emphasized (Hu, 2021; Pei, 2019). However, during the first decade to 2010, EMI teaching was, in the majority, applied in departments of foreign languages education with limited offering in other humanities and social science courses as Hu (2015, p. 55) noted: "There were basically no reports on the applicability of this model to science and engineering students".

The decade since witnessed a steady increase in the number of EMI courses implemented in Chinese universities (Wen, 2020). A study by Mohrmank (2014) identified that the East China Normal University, one of the pioneers of EMI teaching in China, had established the goals of enrolling 5000 international students and 10% of its courses to be offered through EMI. Whilst, "In policy, EMI courses are reported to cultivate student talents, respond to globalisation, promote internationalisation and improve the quality of teaching" (Rose et al., 2020), in practice, many EMI courses in China's higher education institutions are facing difficulties. Research by Xu (2020), reported that the EMI lecturers highlighted their lack of language proficiency and pedagogical expertise as challenges in their EMI teaching. Very little empirical research was identified which explored EMI teaching methods or strategies in the context of course and content development and less have reported actual EMI lecture implementation and current EMI teaching methods in practice (Duan, 2017; Jiang et al., 2019; Lin, 2021).

On reviewing the research literature on EMI, gaps have appeared in the overall research agenda. Firstly, and most importantly the domain of EMI is not clarified. Descriptions of EMI abound, but its boundary is yet to be defined. What does English, Medium or Instruction comprise? Whose English is it in the EMI? How is 'English' in EMI different from that in EFL, ESL or ESP? That these fundamental questions are not asked nor answered leaves EMI teaching and research in a somewhat shambolic state; it leaves knowledge generation of EMI teaching blurry, superficial, convenient and unsystematic. Secondly, epistemological understanding of knowledge construction, of the nature of the knowledge obtainable through research, and the relationship between a researcher and the researched people is yet to be unearthed in the literature reviewed. In conducting research into EMI teaching, it is important to understand and assess the phenomenon through the participants' recollections, description and interpretation in addition to that of the researcher's (Creswell & Clark, 2017) – not in place of the researcher's participation. Whilst it may be convenient to rely on surveys or interviews foregrounding the participants' opinions, attitudes or beliefs, exploring the underlying components of the 'how or what' of EMI is equally, if not, more important. Implementing a research method which includes researchers' participation will secure an intellectual space, informed by their theories, hypotheses, background knowledge and values in knowledge construction. Alhassen (2021, p. 3) supports this argument espousing the benefit of including researcher observations in order to "complement and validate … data". This methodology has been underdeveloped or under reported in the current literature. This book reveals the critical importance of responding to EMI teaching in a context where English hegemony and colonization are becoming more entrenched, and the prevailing research methodology is lagging behind.

## 1.4 The Research Supporting This Book

The research informing this book enlisted a qualitative paradigm to investigate the practices of a cohort of EMI lecturers in a university in Southern China which is actively pursuing an agenda of internationalization. At the time this research was undertaken (2019), more than 10% of student enrolments were from abroad including overseas students with Chinese backgrounds, and 8% of the teaching staff were registered as lecturers of EMI programs across a range of disciplines including Biochemistry, Global Studies, Engineering, Physics, Mathematics, Medical Science, Marketing, Computer Science and Metaphysics. A "single setting case study with multiple sub-cases" (Diop & Liu, 2020, p. 1) was chosen as the most appropriate research design in order to acquire an in-depth understanding of these EMI lecturers' practices within their discipline areas. Whilst locating this research in a single 'real-life' context could be regarded as a limitation in terms of the amount of data collected and generalizability of results, the intention of this research is to provide evidence-based insight to advance the future development and design of contextualized EMI programs. The focus is on the pedagogical issues raised by the EMI lecturers as participants in this complex teaching and learning context, supplemented by the researcher's observations of their EMI, and to a lesser extent, their Chinese Medium Instruction (CMI) teaching. This research is neither an investigation into student attitudes, nor an evaluation of the success or otherwise of the EMI programs in terms of student learning outcomes. The student focus is beyond the scope of this research and its intention to identify evidence-based EMI teaching practice by (1) exploring the pedagogical and instructional characteristics of Chinese background EMI lecturers', (2) identifying teaching strategies implemented (if there were some) to enhance student interaction and engagement, and (3) uncovering examples of

Table 1.1 Summary of data collection protocol

| Data collected | No of participants | Description of data |
| --- | --- | --- |
| Survey | 69 | Data collected around the themes: Lecturer-student reciprocity in their interactions; Understanding of learning and knowledge; Control of knowledge and students' prior knowledge. |
| Observation EMI | 19 | Two hours of observations with each lecturer; these were recorded, and notes taken. |
| Observation CMI | 3 of the 19 | Two hours of observations with each lecturer; these were recorded, and notes taken. |
| Stimulated recall (interview) | 19 | Stimulated recall interviews were conducted on conclusion of the teaching sessions with field notes recorded. The purpose was to seek clarification and explanation from the lecturers around some of the phenomena observed in their teaching. |

linguistic repertoires to provide evidence of how their L1 (Chinese) impacts on their L2 (English) use and how translanguaging practice unfolds in this EMI space.

### 1.4.1 Data Collection

Data were collected over a three-month period and included a qualitative survey, the researcher's observations of the EMI lecturers' practices followed by a stimulated recall (interview), where the participating lecturers were able to discuss issues identified during the lecture observations. Sixty-nine EMI academic staff including professors, associate professors and lecturers completed the survey; 19 of these further accepted the invitation for the researcher to observe their lectures and to participate in a stimulated recall interview. In parallel with their EMI teaching, some of the lecturers offered the same EMI units via Chinese Medium Instruction (CMI) and permission was given from three of the 19 for the researcher to observe their CMI classes. This enabled a reference point when addressing the impact of languages (L1 and L2) on their teaching. The combination of observation and stimulated recall intreviews balanced the participants' and the researcher's contribution to the research. This dual approach allowed "objective tests" as well as "self-reports" (Macaro & Akincioglu, 2018, p. 64). The data collection protocol is represented in the Table 1.1.

## 1.5 Book Structure

This book is structured into eight chapters. Chapter 2 addresses the complexities of EMI and deconstructs the individual E, M and I to ascertain how each contributes to the understanding and conceptualization of the term. It questions and navigates the 'English' from a multilingualism view by proposing that the 'English' of EMI

## 1.5 Book Structure

occurs in bilingual or multilingual contexts and is therefore beyond the entitlements of authenticity and nativism that monolingualism claims. The conceptualization continues by exploring 'Medium' in relation to discourse and how Medium influences and is influenced by the aspects of mode, field and tenor when situated in a particular social and cultural context. This Chapter further conceptualizes 'Instruction' from the standpoints of pedagogy and teaching and learning theories. It contends 'Instruction' represents a set of practical principles based on individual educators' pedagogical positions with reference to and addressing learners' prior knowledge, cognitive need and motivation.

Chapter 3 examines the EMI lecturers' pedagogical alignment and instructional practices. It counters a predominance in the current literature highlighting EMI research on language with less concern on pedagogy, suggesting educators of Confucius heritage tend to implement expository rather than constructivist teaching methods. This Chapter provides an in-depth exposé into the Chinese EMI lecturers' actual classroom teaching and how their individual pedagogical stance has influenced their everyday practice. An exploration of the following questions guides the discussion of the research findings: Do these lecturers who are from the same cultural and educational system share similar pedagogical views and instructional practices? Is the subject area of teaching an impact factor in terms of the lecturers' tendencies or preferences to implement one pedagogy over another? (For example, do lecturers teaching in STEM areas tend to share similar instructional principles compared to those in the humanities, social sciences and education?)

Chapter 4 drills beneath the macro level of pedagogical and instructional analysis, to an investigation of the Chinese EMI lecturers' strategies for engaging students in their EMI programs. Literature reports quality engagement is a key for successful learning, however when lecturers or teachers conduct teaching in English (their second or foreign language), there is often a shortfall in those teachers' repertoire of engagement strategies. The purpose of this Chapter is to examine the Chinese EMI lecturers' engagement portfolio, to respond to two concerns raised in the literature through the questions: Do these EMI lecturers have discernible engagement and interactive activities with students in EMI classes which differ from their CMI strategies? and Is the English as the instructional language, or their pedagogical ideology accountable for any difference? This Chapter is not aspiring to measure the effectiveness that engagement has brought to learning, but rather to capture the characteristics of engagement strategies demonstrated by the EMI lecturers.

Chapter 5 examines the EMI lecturers' instructional language from a psycholinguistic perspective. Data reveal that L1 influence plays a positive, functional role in terms of facilitating EMI lecturers' teaching and students' learning. Theoretically, this Chapter moves beyond a structuralist view of judging language transfer as right or wrong, correct or incorrect, perfect or deficit. It operationalizes a post-structuralist perception by proposing 'explicit' and 'implicit' transfer and acknowledges L1-influenced EMI lecturers' English, as a temporary form of languaging within the translaguaging process.

Chapter 6 centres on the observed instances of the EMI lecturers implementing pragmatic strategies. Effective use of pragmatic strategies provides various types of signposts directing students to logically capture the direction, the transition, the sequence and the comparison in the instruction. This strategy has the potential to challenge the limitation created by 'imperfect' English. This Chapter also focuses on an analysis of the EMI lecturers' use of pragmatic markers (PMs) in their teaching. Acknowledging there were some individual differences, a trend in PM use and the degree of pragmatic transfer revealed in this group's teaching was identified. This prevailing trend can be explained with respect to the EMI lecturers' pedagogical ideology and practice, culturally influenced teacher-student relationships, the EMI subject matter, and the lecturers' language cognition as L2 (English) speakers.

Chapter 7 investigates the Chinese EMI lecturers' position and practice as bilingual educators through a post-structuralist, translanguaging frame of reference. Literature unanimously indicates that translanguaging practices can positively scaffold and facilitate students' learning. This Chapter is prompted by the questions: How is translanguaging practiced in these lecturers' EMI teaching? and How does translanguaging practice reflect their language ideology and identity? Through an analysis of observation and stimulated recall data, this Chapter concludes that the prestigious status of the English language has not been challenged by these EMI lecturers; translanguaging as an advanced concept is yet to be ideologically accepted by the majority of these bilingual professionals; and whist translanguaging appears in some EMI lecturers' practices it was not necessarily fully and positively embraced.

Chapter 8 revisits and recounts the current EMI research literature exposing some major challenges with its trajectory in the field. It reflects on the design of this research, which endeavoured to empower the researcher's role, as a knowledge co-constructor with participants' whilst providing a voice for their understandings of the issues in their own EMI teaching and EMI in general. Finally, this Chapter proposes and shares a framework (Constructivist EMI Teaching Framework) developed in response to insights gleaned from this research and my many years of EMI training experience. This Framework is offered with a hope that it can be a working model for consideration by other EMI educators who aspire to a student-centered, constructivist pedagogy when delivering courses and/or training programs through EMI.

## References

Alhassan, A. (2021). Challenges and professional development needs of EMI lecturers in Omani higher education. *SAGE Open, 1–12.* https://doi.org/10.1177/21582440211061527

Ament, J. R., & Pérez-Vidal, C. (2015). Linguistic outcomes of English medium instruction programmes in higher education: A study on economics undergraduates at a Catalan university. *Higher Learning Research Communications, 5,* 47–68.

Arabaski, J., & Wojtaszek, A. (2015). *Individual learner differences in SLA.* Multilingual Matters. https://doi.org/10.21832/9781847694355.

Arnó-Macià, E., & Mancho-Barés, G. (2015). The role of content and language in content and language integrated learning (CLIL) at university. *English for Specific Purposes, 37,* 63–73. https://doi.org/10.1016/j.esp.2014.06.007

# References

Basturkmen, H. (2018). Dealing with language issues during subject teaching in EMI: The perspectives of two accounting lecturers. *TESOL Quarterly, 52*, 692–700.

Björkman, B. (2016). English-medium instruction and English as the lingua franca in higher education in central and northern Europe. In M.-L. Pitzl & R. Osimk-Dale (Eds.), *English as a Lingua Franca: Perspective and prospects* (pp. 57–68). Ulrike Jessner, Claire Kramsh, De Gruyter Mouton.

Bologna Declaration. (1999). *Joint declaration of the European Ministers of Education Convened in Bologna*. http://www.magna-charta.org/resources/files/BOLOGNA_DECLARATION.pdf.

Brüning C., & Purrmann, M-S. (2014). CLIL pedagogy in Europe: CLIL teacher education in Germany. In C. Bruning & M.-S. Purrmann (Eds.), *English as a foreign language teacher education* (pp. 313–338). https://doi.org/10.1163/9789401210485_018.

Bunce, P., Phillipson, V. R., Rapatahana, V., & Ruanni, F. (Eds.). (2016). *Why English? confronting the Hydra*. Multilingual Matters.

Chen, S., & Tsai, Y. (2012). Research on English teaching and learning. *Language Teaching, 45*, 180–201.

Chen, J., & Yu, Y. (2018). An EMI current situation research for non-English major students – A case of Central South University. *Journal of Innovation and Enterprise Education, 4*, 104–108. DOI: CNKI: SUN; CXYC.0.2018-04-025. [陈洁 & 于雨田. (2018). 面向非英语专业学生的EMI英语教学现状研究 – 以中南大学为例. 创新与创业教育(04),104-108. DOI: CNKI: SUN: CXYC.0.2018-04-025].

Chen, H., Han, J., & Wright, D. (2020). Focussing language and pedagogy: A case study of English as a medium of instruction in a Chinese University. *Sustainability, 12*(4046), 1–16. https://doi.org/10.3390/su12104046

Costa, F., & Coleman, J. (2013). A survey of English-medium instruction in Italian higher education. *International Journal of Bilingual Education, 16*, 3–19.

Cots, J. (2012). Introducing English-medium instruction at the University of Lleida, Spain. In A. Doiz, D. Lasagabaster, & J. Sierra (Eds.), *English medium instruction at universities: Global challenges* (pp. 106–128). Multilingual Matters.

Coyle, D., Hood, P., & Marsh, D. (2010). *CLIL*. Cambridge University Press.

Creswell, J., & Clark, V. (2017). *Designing and conducting mixed methods research*. Sage Publications.

Dalton-Puffer, C. (2013). A construct of cognitive discourse functions for conceptualising content-language integration in CLIL and multilingual education. *European Journal of Applied Linguists, 1*, 216–253.

De Cillia, R., & Schweiger, T. (2001). English as a language of instruction at Austrian Universities. In U. Ammon (Ed.), *The dominance of English as a language of science: Effects on other languages and language communities* (pp. 363–388). De Gruyter Mouto. https://doi.org/10.1515/9783110869484.363

De Wit, H., Hunter, F., Howard, L. & Egron-Polak, E. (2015). Internationalisation of higher education. *European Union*. http://www.europarl.europa.eu/studies. DOI: https://doi.org/10.2861/444393.

Dearden, J. (2014). *English as a medium of instruction – A growing global phenomenon; interim report*. University of Oxford.

Dearden, J. (2015). *English as a medium of instruction – A growing global phenomenon*. http://www.britishcouncil.org/education/ihe/knowledge-centre/english-language-higher-education/report-english medium-instruction. Accessed 15 Aug 2021.

Dearden, J., & Macaro, E. (2016). Higher education teachers' attitudes towards English medium instruction: A three-country comparison. *Studies in Second Language Learning and Teaching, 3*, 455–486.

Dimova, S., Hultgren, A., & Jensen, C. (Eds.). (2015). *English-medium instruction in higher education in Europe*. Mouton de Gruyter.

Diop, K. A. S., & Liu, E. (2020). Categorization of case in case study research method: New approach. *Knowledge & Performance Management, 4*(1), 1–14. https://doi.org/10.21511/kpm.04(1).2020.01

Doiz, A., & Lasagabaster, D. (2018). Teachers' and students' second language motivational self system in English medium instruction: A qualitative approach. *TESOL Quarterly, 52*, 657–679.

Doiz, A., Lasagabaster, D., & Sierra, J. (2012). Introduction. In A. Doiz, D. Lasagabaster, & J. Sierra (Eds.), *English medium instruction at universities: Global challenges* (pp. xvii–xxii). Multilingual Matters.

Duan, D. (2017). Literature review on English-medium instruction at home and abroad. *Journal of Architectural Education in Institutions of Higher Learning, 4*, 94–99. [段丹阳 (2017). 全英教学研究综述.高等建筑教育, 4, 94–99].

Ersheidat, G., & Tahir, H. (2020). Genetic relationship among languages: An overview. *International Journal of Language Education and Applied Linguistics, 10*(1), 17–27. https://doi.org/10.15282/ijleal.v10.3320

González Ardeo, J. (2013). (In)compatibility of CLIL and ESP courses at university. *Language Value, 5*, 24–47.

Goodman, B., Kambatyrova, A., Aitzhanova, K., Kerimkulova, S., & Chsherbakov, A. (2022). Institutional supports for language development through English-medium instruction: A factor analysis. *TESOL Quarterly, 56*(2).

Gu, J., Ma, C., Zhu, C., & Chen, G. (2020). A discussion of EMI teaching mode for a subject basic course. *Industrial & Science Tribune, 19*(5), 173–174. https://doi.org/10.3969/j.issn.1673-5641.2020.05.088. [辜姣, 马超群, 朱纯, & 陈国庆. (2020). 专业基础课EMI课程教学模式探讨.产业与科技论坛, 19(5), 173–174. doi: 10.3969/j.issn.1673-5641.2020.05.088].

Gunnarsson, T., Housen, A., van de Weijer, J., & Källkvist, M. (2015). Multilingual students' self-reported use of their language repertoires when writing in English. *Apples-Journal of Applied Language Studies, 9*(1), 1–21.

Gustafson, H. (2018). Capturing EMI teachers' linguistic needs: A usage-based perspective. *International Journal of Bilingual Education and Bilingualism, 23*(9), 1071–1082. https://doi.org/10.1080/13670050.2018.14253671071-1082

He, J., & Chiang, S. (2016). Challenges to English-medium instruction (EMI) for international students in China. *English Today, 32*, 63–67.

Hu, Z. (2015). A long way to go for internationalization of higher education: Introduction of A cross discipline research of EMI in higher education institutions. *Foreign Languages Research, 6*, 53–55. doi: https://doi.org/10.13978/j.cnki.wyyj.2015.06.010. [胡壮麟 (2015). 高等教育国际化任重道远 – 读《高校全英语教学模式(EMI)的超学科研究》. 外语研究, (06), 53–55. doi:10.13978/j.cnki.wyyj.2015.06.010].

Hu, H. (2021). Strategic moves for internationalization of education: An introduction of "A study of the EMI capability of lecturers in Chinese universities". *Shandong Foreign Language Teaching, 1*, 132–135. doi: https://doi.org/10.16482/j.sdwy37-1026.2021-01-014. [胡壮麟 (2021). 教育国际化的战略举措 – 《中国高校教师全英语教学(EMI)能力研究》评介. 山东外语教学(01), 132–135. doi:10.16482/j.sdwy37-1026.2021-01-014].

Hu, G., & Lei, J. (2014a). English-medium instruction at a Chinese university: rhetoric and reality. *Language Policy, 13*(1), 21–40.

Hu, G., & Lei, J. (2014b). English-medium instruction in Chinese higher education. *Higher Education, 67*, 551–567.

Huang, D., & Singh, M. (2014). Critical perspectives on testing teaching. *Asia-Pacific Journal of Teacher Education, 42*(4), 363–378. https://doi.org/10.1080/1359866X.2014.956046

Ismailov, M., Chiu, T., Dearden, J., Yamamoto, Y., & Djalilova, N. (2021). Challenges to internationalisation of university programmes: A systematic thematic synthesis of qualitative research on learner-centred English Medium Instruction (EMI) pedagogy. *Sustainability, 13*, 12642. https://doi.org/10.3390/su1322126

# References

Jenkins, J. (2018). The internationalization of higher education: But what about its lingua franca? In M. Kumiko (Ed.), *English-medium instruction from an English as a Lingua Franca perspective: Exploring the higher education context* (pp. 15–31). Routledge.

Jiang, L., Zhang, L., & May, S. (2019). Implementing English-medium instruction (EMI) in China: Teachers' practices and perceptions, and students' learning motivation and needs. *International Journal of Bilingual Education and Bilingualism, 22*(2), 107–119. https://doi.org/10.1080/13670050.2016.1231166

Kachru, B. (1985). Standards, codification and sociolinguistic realism: The English language in the outer circle. In R. Quirk & H. G. Widdowson (Eds.), *English in the world: Teaching and learning the language and literatures* (pp. 11–30). Cambridge University Press.

Kampen, E., Admiraal, W., & Berry, A. (2018). Content and language integrated learning in the Netherlands: Teachers' self-reported pedagogical practices. *International Journal of Bilingual Education and Bilingualism, 21*, 222–236.

Kim, K. (2011). Korean professor and student perceptions of the efficacy of English-medium instruction. *Linguistic Research, 28*(3), 711–741.

Kim, J., Choi, J., & Tatar, B. (2017a). English-medium instruction and intercultural sensitivity: A Korean case study. *Journal of Studies in International Education., 21*(5), 467–482. https://doi.org/10.1177/1028315317720767

Kim, E., Kweon, S.-O., & Kim, J. (2017b). Korean engineering students' perceptions of English-medium instruction (EMI) and L1 use in EMI classes. *Journal of Multilingual and Multicultural Development, 38*(2), 1–16. https://doi.org/10.1080/01434632.2016.1177061

Kling, J. 2013. *Teacher identity in English-Medium instruction: Teacher cognitions from a Danish tertiary education context*. University of Copenhagen dissertation.

Kumiko, M. (2018). Exploring EMI in higher education from an ELF perspective. In M. Kumiko (Ed.), *English-medium instruction from an English as a lingua franca perspective: Exploring the higher education context* (pp. 1–11). Routledge.

Kuteeva, M., & Airey, J. (2014). Disciplinary differences in the use of English in higher education: Reflections on recent language policy developments. *Higher Education, 67*(5), 533–549.

Lasagabaster, D. (2018). Fostering team teaching: Mapping out a research agenda for English-medium instruction at university level. *Language Teaching; Cambridge, 51*(3), 400–416.

Lee, J.-W., & Lee, H. (2018). Human capital and income inequality. *Journal of Asia Pacific Economy, 23*(4), 554–583.

Lin, L. (2021). Bridging the gap of language and content in english-mediated instruction: Pedagogy in English literature course. *Journal of Higher Education Research, 3*, 110–120. doi: CNKI: SUN: GJYJ.0.2021-03-018. [林丽云 (2021). 语言和课程内容的融合 – 以"英文文学"课程为例的全英课程教学方法探讨. 高等教育研究学报(03), 110–120. doi: CNKI: SUN: GJYJ.0.2021-03-018].

Lin, A., & Lo, Y. (2017). Trans/languaging and the triadic dialogue in content and language integrated learning (CLIL) classrooms. *Language and Education, 31*, 26–45.

Liu, D. (2020). Exploring and implementing constructivist learning activities in english medium instruction courses: A case study of EMI management teaching. *The Guide of Science & Education 29*, 123–126. DOI:10.16400/j.cnki.kjdkz.2020.10.058. [刘丹 (2020). 运用建构主义主动学习模式改善EMI课堂教学的探索与实践 – 以管理学原理教学为例. 科教导刊(中旬刊) (29), 123–126. doi:10.16400/j.cnki.kjdkz.2020.10.058].

Ljosland, R. (2014). Language planning confronted by everyday communication in the international university: The Norwegian case. *Journal of Multilingual and Multicultural Development, 35*(4), 392–405.

Macaro, E., & Akincioglu, M. (2018). Turkish university students' perceptions about English medium instruction: Exploring year group, gender and university type as variables. *Journal of Multilingual and Multicultural Development, 39*(3), 256–270.

Mancho-Barés, G., & Arnó-Macià, E. (2017). EMI lecturer training programmes and academic literacies. *ESP Today, 5*, 266–290.

MOET. (2008). *Teaching and learning foreign languages in the national education system, period 2008 to 2020*. MOET Decision, No. 1400/QD-TTg. https://www.scribd.com/document/386798302/.

Mohrmank, K. (2014). East China Normal University education in the Lead. Portraits of 21st century Chinese Universities. *China Quarterly, 217*(4), 201–204.

Mortensen, J. (2014). Language policy from below: Language choice in student project groups in a multilingual university setting. *Journal of Multilingual and Multicultural Development, 35*(4), 425–442.

Muguruza, B., Cenoz, J., & Gorter, D. (2020). Implementing translanguaging pedagogies in an English medium instruction course. *International Journal of Multilingualism*. https://doi.org/10.1080/14790718.2020.1822848

Mühleisen, S. (2003). Towards global diglossia? In C. Mair (Ed.), *The politics of English as a world language: New horizons in postcolonial cultural studies* (pp. 107–118). Rodopi.

O'Dowd, R. (2018). The training and accreditation of teachers for English medium instruction: An overview of practice in European universities. *International Journal of Bilingual Education and Bilingualism, 21*, 553–563.

Pei, X. (2019). The study of education ecological development of EMI teaching competencies in China's Universities. *Tribune of Education Culture, 11*(1), 75–78. [裴欣欣 (2019). 我国高校EMI教师教学胜任力生态化发展. 教育文化论坛, 11(1), 75–78].

Phan, T. (2022). *Content and Language Integrated Learning (CLIL): A case study of lecturers' experiences of professional learning for Engineering and English Integrated Learning Program within Vietnamese Higher Education*. Upublished PhD thesis Western Sydney University, Australia: Penrith, Sydney, NSW.

Phillipson, R. (2006). English, a cuckoo in the European higher education nest of languages? *European Journal of English Studies, 10*(1), 13–32.

Phillipson, R. (2017). Myths and realities of 'global' English. *Language Policy, 16*, 313–331.

Phillipson, R. (2018). Foreword. In R. Bernard & Z. Hasim (Eds.), *English medium instruction programs: Perspectives from South East Asian Universities*. Routledge.

Quan, W., Chen, B., & Shu, F. (2017). Publish or impoverish: An investigation of the monetary reward system of science in China (1999-2016). *Aslib Journal of Information Management, 69*(5), 486–502. https://doi.org/10.1108/AJIM-01-2017-0014

Ren, Y. (2016). The future direction for internationalising higher education under the double first class plan. *Journal of China Higher Education*, http://plan.njau.edu.cn/info/1094/1825.htm.

Rose, H., McKinley, J., Xu, X., & Zhou, S. (2020). *Investigating policy and implementation of Engoish-medium instruction in higher education institutions in China: A report by EMI Oxford research group in collaboration with the British Council in China*. British Council.

Sah, P., & Li, G. (2022). Translanguaging or unequal languaging? Unfolding the plurilingual discourse of English medium instruction policy in Nepal's public schools. *International Journal of Bilingual Education and Bilingualism, 25*(6), 2075–2094.

Shohamy, E. (2012). A critical perspective on the use of English as a medium of instruction at universities. In A. Doiz, D. Lasagabaster, & J. Sierra (Eds.), *English medium instruction at universities: Global challenges* (pp. 196–213). Multilingual Matters.

Tai, K., & Li, W. (2021). Constructing playful talk through Translanguaging in English medium instruction mathematics classroom. *Applied Linguistics, 42*(4), 607–640.

Tsou, W., & Kao, S. (Eds.). (2017). *English as a medium of instruction in higher education implementations and classroom practices in Taiwan*. Springer.

Wächter, B., & Maiworm, F. (2014). *English-taught programmes in European higher education: The state of play in 2014*. Lemmens.

Wen, X. (2020). Exploring the impact of English medium instruction on Chinese university students' academic achievement: A comparison between EMI and CMI. *Journal of Shangrao Normal University, 1*, 113–120. doi: CNKI:SUN:SRSX.0.2020-01-001. [温湘频 (2020). 测试视角下地方高校EMI与CMI教学效果实证研究. 上饶师范学院学报, (01), 113–120. doi: CNKI:SUN:SRSX.0.2020-01-001].

## References

Werther, C., Denver, L., Jensen, C., & Mees, I. (2014). Using English as a medium of instruction at university level in Denmark: The lecturer's perspective. *Journal of Multilingual and. Multicultural Development, 35*, 443–462.

Wilkinson, R. (2012). English-medium instruction at a Dutch University: Challenges and pitfalls. In A. Doiz, D. Lasagabaster, & J. Sierra (Eds.), *English medium instruction at universities: Global challenges* (pp. 3–26). Multilingual Matters.

Wilkinson, R., & Zegers, V. (2008). Introduction. In R. Wilkinson & V. Zegers (Eds.), *Realizing content and language integration in higher education* (pp. 1–9). Maastricht University.

Wilson, K., & Devereux, L. (2014). Scaffolding theory: High challenge, high support in academic language and learning contexts. *Journal of Academic Language Learning, 8*, 91–100.

Xu, J. (2020). Research on the reform of EMI teaching mode in colleges and universities under ISEC program. *Journal of Chifeng University (Philosophy and Social Science Chinese Edition), 5,* 107–111. doi:10.13398/j.cnki.issn1673-2596.2020.05.025. [徐婧 (2020). ISEC项目下的高校EMI课程教学模式改革研究. 赤峰学院学报(汉文哲学社会科学版)(05), 107–111. doi:10.13398/j.cnki.issn1673-2596.2020.05.025].

Xu, Y. (2021). Challenges and suggested approaches for EMI content lecturers in the context of Chinese State Universities. *BCP Education & Psychology, 3*, 84–89.

**Open Access** This chapter is licensed under the terms of the Creative Commons Attribution 4.0 International License (http://creativecommons.org/licenses/by/4.0/), which permits use, sharing, adaptation, distribution and reproduction in any medium or format, as long as you give appropriate credit to the original author(s) and the source, provide a link to the Creative Commons license and indicate if changes were made.

The images or other third party material in this chapter are included in the chapter's Creative Commons license, unless indicated otherwise in a credit line to the material. If material is not included in the chapter's Creative Commons license and your intended use is not permitted by statutory regulation or exceeds the permitted use, you will need to obtain permission directly from the copyright holder.

# Chapter 2
# Conceptualization of English Medium Instruction

**Abstract** When exploring English Medium Instruction (EMI) as a concept, the dominant paradigm in the literature pertains to descriptive statements rather than definitions; appears to replicate more of the same and is based on what could be labeled 'convenient' studies. EMI research designed for change and innovation, aiming to propose solutions or generate frameworks for improvement in practice, is wanting. This Chapter addresses the complexities of EMI through the multiple lenses of theory and deconstructs EMI's individual elements to ascertain how each contributes to its understanding and conceptualization. The 'English' in EMI teaching is situated within bi/multilingual contexts. It extends beyond its Anglophone authenticity, thus is a plural form responding to crosslinguistic influence and translanguaging practice. The 'Medium' is a 'channel' through which teaching occurs and often involves multimedia technology. It influences and is influenced by mode, field, tenor and context. The 'Instruction' is theorized as a set of principles encapsulating EMI lecturers' pedagogical stance and reflects how they position the learners. Moving beyond the general, simplistic descriptions of EMI prevalent in the literature, this Chapter aims to provide a conceptual framework of EMI to inform the data analysis in subsequent Chapters.

**Keywords** English · Englishes · Crosslinguistic influence · Translanguaging · Medium · Channel · QAIT model · The first principles of instruction

## 2.1 Introduction

Su Shi (1037–1101), a Song Dynasty poet, once visited Lushan Mountain (in Eastern China) and wrote a poem titled "Ti Xi Lin Bi" (Written on the Wall at West Forest Temple) describing his impression of the mountain. It was later translated by an American, *Barton Watson as:*

> From the side, a whole range; from the end, a single peak;
> Far, near, high, low, no two parts alike;
> Why can't I tell the true shape of Lushan?
> Because I myself am in the mountain (Su Shi, the author, cited in Watson, 1993)

This poem conveys an enlightened philosophical message. That is, seeing the world from multiple angles positions the viewer above and beyond a direct, straight line to a unilateral view. Enacting a multidimensional viewing platform can reduce biased opinions and generate more objective and complete conclusions. This notion of assigning multiple lenses to view the world can be applied to EMI. From the side, the end, the high and low, each angle enlightens the viewer with one particular aspect of EMI, however a full and complete picture of what constitutes EMI, requires the viewer to appraise and combine multiple meanings to produce a viable and workable understanding of EMI as a concept. Understanding the conceptual meaning of EMI, requires an unpacking of the 'English', the 'Medium' and the 'Instruction'. Conceptualizing EMI through this approach has the potential to move EMI boldly forward, towards developing a framework of possibilities for improving successful EMI teaching and learning.

## 2.2 Conceptualizing 'ENGLISH' in EMI

Two theoretical lenses through which to view the 'English' in EMI are monolingualism and multilingualism. Monolingual advocates view the 'English' in EMI as holding a virtuous, powerful role, synonymous with 'English only', and therefore unrelated to any other language operating within the context of EMI teaching and learning. The Chinese equivalent to this monolingual view is *quan ying shou ke* (*quan*: absolute, pure; *ying*: English, *shou ke*: teaching), or 'teaching totally in English'. This statement reflects and reinforces the vision of EMI as a monolingual concept. Multilingualism, however, acknowledges educators and learners participating in EMI programs are bilinguals who must navigate and negotiate the relationship between English, their second language (L2) and their first language (L1).

Analogous to English as a Foreign Language (EFL) or English as a Second Language (ESL), EMI is then delegated into the non-native category as it is implemented by teaching professionals from a bi- or multilingual background with English as an additional language. This view does not engage with the notion that, in this circumstance, the English as L2, comprises only part of the language expertise or repertoire of any bi/multilingual teacher. The difference between EMI and EFL/ESL is that the 'English' in EMI is not a key learning outcome in and of itself. It is rather a 'side' product when compared to the importance of content knowledge and skills. In EMI the English acts primarily as a medium or a communication channel and its functional role can be achieved in the absence of 'perfect' English but in the presence of, a variety of Englishes or World Englishes (Kachru & Nelson, 1996). This is not to argue that EMI lecturers should not aspire to presenting their lessons in good quality English; it needs to be acknowledged that student understanding of the content should not be compromised by an over compliance with formal, over exaggerated, grammatically correct English (Coyle, 2007). There needs to be a space to move beyond aspiring to replicate native-English speaking as the norm in EMI teaching and learning.

## 2.2.1 Should Native English Be the Norm for EMI Lecturers?

Aspirations to achieve native English or 'Anglo-phone' English may be highly desirable among EMI lecturers according to the current literature. For lecturers committed to a monolingual view, they may feel compelled to compare their English with that of native Anglophones (Murahata et al., 2016). For them, replicating Anglophone English and simulating pedagogy of an Anglophone education system might be an ideal benchmark from which to define successful EMI teaching. From this perspective, native English would be essential as a model, a goal, or an inspiration (Davies, 1996; Trimbur, 2008). However, EMI lecturers are charged with the responsibility to impart subject knowledge as the key objective and focus, for teaching in an EMI program. In this regard, the content knowledge should receive most emphasis and English, as the means of communication, should not be given the same power (Coyle, 2007). How EMI lecturers balance the dichotomy between teaching content and purity of the English is often a matter related to their ideology. It needs to be recapped that content and subject knowledge should not be sacrificed by an over emphasis on achieving perfect English presentations. Instilling an expectation in EMI lecturers to adhere to a goal of producing native English as the norm in EMI classrooms is neither desirable nor realistically achievable.

## 2.2.2 Is It 'English' or 'Englishes' in EMI?

As EMI teaching is implemented around the globe, the EMI lecturers' L1 may be genetically close to or quite distant from English. This has led to an interest in considering the various effects of an L1 on the use of English in EMI contexts (Jarvis & Pavlenko, 2008). Ringbom (2006) proposed three categories of cross-linguistic relationships which can be used to explain the reality for EMI lecturers in terms of the influences between L1 and L2. L1s and English considered to have a 'similarity relation/ship' are those derived from the same language origin, for example, Germanic inherited Scandinavian languages and English. An EMI lecturer who operates across such related languages is advantaged by having some shared, similar cognates in crosslinguistic form and meaning. For those whose L1 and English have moderate or little functional and semantic relations such as Sino-Tibetan languages, the L1 can alleviate minor difficulties in EMI teaching. Chinese EMI lecturers' L1, which is regarded having a 'zero relation/ship' (Ringbom, 2006) with English, can still be expected to have some influence on the English in their EMI in phonetic, structural, conceptual and functional areas. Therefore, the 'English' in EMI takes on a plural form with variations world-wide depending on the genetic (crosslinguistic) similarities between the users' L1 and English. As such there is not and cannot be, a universal linguistic framework for EMI.

The 'English' of EMI lecturers is not static, evolving into a dynamic existence intertwining with their L1. When teaching, EMI lecturers do not compartmentalize their two languages into separate and parallel spaces. They could be expected to translanguage, or inherently integrate or move between their two (or more) languages based on the needs of their communication with students. The boundary between EMI lecturers' L1 and English are fluid, as is the case with EFL or ESL lecturers, and there is no clear-cut demarcation between these, but rather a languaging continuum (Garcia, 2009). For EMI lecturers, their L1 would continually supplement their English to assist communication and understanding. It can be that their L1 merges into their English in inventive ways at the language expression level, creation of hybrids and undefined forms for negotiations (Shohamy, 2011). It can also be that L1 is integrated into L2 for assisting cognitive thinking. Following interdependence theory (Cummins, 2001), EMI lecturers' highly proficient L1 can facilitate their own and perhaps their students' thinking and comprehension during EMI classes.

### 2.2.3 Translanguaging – The Nature of EMI Teaching

The dynamic relationship between EMI lecturers' L1 and English determines the nature of the translanguaging experiences in their EMI classes. Translanguaging as post-structuralist theory, acknowledges that bilingual speakers have repertoires of combined resources including knowledge from two languages along with their associated social and cultural backgrounds from which to engage learners. It challenges the conservative language hegemony of monolingualism, and structuralist views of bilinguals occupying two concurrent monolingual spaces and thus living in two separate language worlds (Canagarajah, 2011; Cummins, 2001; Douglas Fir Group, 2016, p. 35; Kubota, 2013; Roy & Galiev, 2011). When language use can be conceptualized as going beyond the language itself, it opens the dialogue on whether EMI needs an insulated single-language conduit to be successful. Perceiving the integration of languages as a 'deficit', itself becomes a deficit from a translanguaging perspective. The conceptualization of translanguaging assigns bi/multilingual teachers or lecturers a legitimate status (García & Li, 2014) within which they are afforded a new teaching and learning reality where the potential resources provided by multiple languages is seen as a significant benefit. This post-structuralist perception allows translanguaging practices to be developed into useful pedagogical practices (Garcia, 2009; Shohamy, 2011). EMI classes are situated in two different, yet interdependent lingual worlds. Hybridity of language use by EMI lecturers has the potential to better facilitate students' learning as translanguaging empowers a "systematic, strategic, affiliative, and sense-making process" (Gutierrez et al., 2001, p. 128). Therefore, there is merit for translanguaging to be practiced intentionally and purposefully as opposed to randomly – for pedagogical reasons and educational purposes.

## 2.3 The 'MEDIUM' in EMI

Within the current EMI literature, 'medium' is a taken for granted concept and is yet to be comprehensively defined. Dearden (2014, p. 4) describes EMI as "the use of the English language to teach academic subjects…". To dissect this overall description further, the 'Medium' could be consigned to the words: "the use of". However, if the 'how' to use is contemplated, then this definition leaves a large open space for people to imagine and interpret. According to Denise Murray (1988, p. 353) in the article *"The context of oral and written language: A framework for mode and medium switching"*, 'medium' is described as the "established methods of communication through language". With reference to EMI, this would equate to 'established methods of communication through English'. Figure 2.1 provides an overview of the components of the 'Medium' in EMI to assist in understanding its conceputalization.

Advancing the concept of 'medium' in EMI as the established 'methods of communication' through English, with reference to a teaching context, these 'methods of communication' could include face-to-face and tele-virtual interactions where teachers and students interact synchronously, or via alternatives such as physical pen and paper or electronic written communication where there may be no immediacy to the interaction – labeled as asynchronous. Although EMI teaching can include the asynchronous written modes (for example, unit modules) it is notable that current EMI research has been focusing on classroom teaching episodes that are delivered in the oral mode through visual and aural channels when lecturers and students are in the same physical or virtual space. The more traditional oral modes of explanation, discussion or speeches appear to dominate the EMI research landscape.

To further comprehend 'medium', the contribution of two related terms, 'channel' and 'mode', are acknowledged. Whilst associated with 'medium', 'channel' has an element of modality whereas 'medium' does not. It has "the pretheoretical sensory modalities" (Murray, 1988, p. 353) such as visual, aural, and tactile channels. For example, written language involves the visual and tactile channels and oral language is processed through the visual and aural channels. Hence medium is a broader term, which includes and relies on an appropriate channel to enable successful communication. Comparatively, 'mode' is "specific communication types within a medium" (Murray, 1988, p. 353); it is "a socially shaped and culturally given semiotic resource for making meaning", such as image, writing, gesture, speech, and soundtrack used in representation and communication (Kress, 2010, p. 79). Thus, medium is the tool or platform through which communication occurs and mode refers to the type of communication itself. For example, the mode through a face-to-face synchronous medium can be oral, including conversation, group discussions or debates, or alternatively one person's speech, explanation or report. When an asynchronous medium is implemented, the mode could be written, such as email communications, text messages, physical mail, a discussion paper or a document review. In this way, mode is somewhat similar to 'genre', yet different in that

**MEDIUM**
The platform through which communication occurs

Synchronous
(physical and virtual face to face)
(immediacy of communication}

Asynchronous
(lags between communication and response)

Oral Mode

Written Mode (or Oral Recording)

|  | Oral Mode | Written Mode (or Oral Recording) |
|---|---|---|
| **Mode**<br>The specific type of communication | • Conversation<br>• Group discussions/debates<br>• One person speeches/<br>• Explanations<br>• Reports | • Emails<br>• Text messages<br>• Letters<br>• Discussion papers<br>• Reviews<br>• Recorded lecture |
| **Field**<br>Area of study / processes and activities | • Knowledge of the Discipline expressed through oral language | • Knowledge of the Discipline expressed through written language<br>   ○ Lecture Notes<br>   ○ Readings |
| **Tenor**<br>Relationship between participants in communication | • Formal speech<br>• Informal speech | • Personal writing style<br>• Impersonal writing style |
| **Context**<br>The site where communication takes place | • Micro level<br>• Time Place Participants<br>   ○ Individuals<br>   ○ Groups<br>   ○ Classrooms | • Macro level<br>• Institutional, Social, Cultural and Political environments<br>   ○ Rules<br>   ○ Laws<br>   ○ Affiliation |

**Fig. 2.1** Mapping the 'medium' in EMI

it does not narrowly align with a specific literary discourse such as narrative, procedure or information report only (Murray, 1988).

### 2.3.1 Impacts of Medium on Language Use

Synchronous and asynchronous mediums divert or generally divide, communication into oral and written modes. These two modes by themselves are neither alternative nor equivalent to each other. They differ profoundly in function and structure. Synchronous medium supports immediate interaction between communicators thus promoting a consciousness for speakers to be psychologically close to their listeners. It also provides opportunities for audience participation and reactions to be noted, thus flexibility in language use and tailoring the discourse to suit the audience's needs is possible (Rubin, 1987, p. 9).

A synchronous medium of instruction allows teachers or lecturers to spontaneously construct and refine their presentation (Berger & Iyengar, 2013). Thus redundancy, repetition and paraphrasing may occur. This may be especially the case in EMI teaching when lecturers are using English as their additional language in the classroom. This phenomenon can also be viewed as having a positive function as "orality in language is a primary factor contributing to listenability" (Rubin, 1987, p. 9). Redundancy or repetition in the lecturers' talk may ease their concern to keep the lesson flowing and the subject matter highlighted. At the same time the students are afforded more time to keep pace with the lesson and process information when the English and/or environmental barriers hamper understanding. That is, this repetition may provide the listeners with a second chance to recover lost meaning.

A synchronous medium of instruction has the potential to lead to more engagement with students but may be less rigorous in content integration (Chafe, 1985; Rubin, 1987). The teachers or lecturers can easily personalize the communication and actively construct and deconstruct the content. Their potential for real-time composing may result in less density when elaborating information or content, and information may be less compressed compared to an asynchronous medium. In general, synchronous communication is context dependent. To analyse EMI lecturers' classroom teaching, it will be useful to examine how or whether the lecturers involve the students through the type of personal and emotive language incorporated, how they unpack the information and to what extent they integrate the teaching content.

### 2.3.2 Medium in Relation to Mode, Field, Tenor and Context

The mode or the specific type of communication enacted within the medium is influenced by field, tenor and context (Halliday, 1999; Kress, 2010; Murray, 1988). Field is the discipline or subject matter including its processes or activities within which the language is embedded. In an EMI class, it can be predicted that the subject matter has necessitated a more formal academic spoken or written mode. Thus, the characteristics of the field contribute to the choice of mode within the medium. In reverse, an example that medium or mode impacts on field would be when the same message is forwarded to the same person via a text message and also via a printed letter. In this instance, the linguistic choice is adjustable due to the characteristics of the two different fields and modes.

Tenor or the interpersonal relationship between speaker and audience affects mode. The choice or switch of mode can reflect how the speaker views and positions the audience and how s/he wants to be viewed by the audience (Halliday, 1999; Traugott & Romaine, 1985). Tenor in language exchanges can provide evidence of the relative power relationship between participants. In an EMI class, some lecturers may aspire to teach from a position of power and authority in the teacher/student relationship and consequently may prefer to use language with a formal (enforces a distance from the students), direct lecturing style. Tenor displayed this way may also be reinforced by the institutional identities and policies and may also align with the field being taught.

Contexts, particularly at the macro level, are often considered to be quite stable. Take a specific educational institution as an example. In that context, lecturers become very adept at adjusting the language mode of their teaching in response to established institutional support or constraints and broader community needs and expectations. However, for EMI programs around the globe, EMI lecturers from different countries are situated in varied contexts – that differ in institutional, cultural, social, and political ideologies. These different contexts will influence how the EMI lecturers will cross languages and culture, and switch language codes according to their contexts. For EMI research, the context, including individuals, classrooms, institutions and countries all impact as significant factors when exploring medium in EMI programs.

In summary, whilst analysing the 'medium' in EMI, it is important to investigate its relationship to, and how it is constituted by mode, field, tenor and context. Decisions on what will constitute the 'medium' in EMI lectures will depend on the interaction among the desired attributes from each of the categories. A shift in the medium or mode of communication impacts on the other contributors (field, tenor and context) and vice versa.

## 2.4 The 'INSTRUCTION' in EMI

Similar to 'Medium', there is scant literature contributing to an understanding of 'instruction' within the realm of EMI. To consider Dearden's (2014, p. 3) definition of EMI where 'instruction' is explained as "to teach academic subjects", to clarify the nature, meaning and characteristics of "to teach…" may help establish EMI's pedagogical domain and distinguish it from language-focused ESL or EAL teaching. Research into EMI teaching needs to be enhanced by examining the underlying instructional system and its prevailing pedagogical principles – a current void.

## 2.4 The 'INSTRUCTION' in EMI

Positivist advocates believe instruction is a set of subject/content-oriented rules or principles that should be followed in practice. It is described as collective techniques of selection, sequence, pacing, evaluation criteria and "the discursive rules which characterize the practice" (Morais, 1999, p. 40). According to Hyun (2006, p. 137, 144) such rules, if they could be, should be "timeless truths" and "laws" for delivering knowledge. By following such a direct process, teachers or lecturers are able to manipulate the environment of an individual learner so that "his [sic] [learning] behavior is changed in a specified way" (Tennyson & Merrill, 1971, p. 28). A teaching effort can then "lead the learner in a certain direction to achieve planned goals and objectives" (Hyun, 2006, p. 137). It is thus a mechanical, lock step, linear process (Eisner, 1994). Such views of instruction appear to align the classroom teaching of students to conducting experiments in laboratories. In contrast, pedagogy includes "something extra" (Biesta & Miedema, 2002, p. 177).

In actual teaching and learning contexts, instruction goes beyond the objective/s of delivering a lesson itself. Lecturers plan their lectures with due consideration to their students as well as their own teaching ideology and pedagogical preference. From the perspective of learning theory, Slavin (1995, p. 166) argues that educators must attend to and adapt "instruction to students' levels of knowledge", motivating and monitoring their learning, and managing their behavior. He proposed the QAIT (Quality, Appropriateness, Incentive, Time) model of instruction for achieving effective learning outcomes. By *Quality of Instruction,* he refers to the degree to which information or skills are presented whereby students are able to comprehend new knowledge; *Appropriate Levels of Instruction* is concerned with how best to structure "the instruction to the range of the students' levels of prior knowledge and learning rates" (p. 168); *Incentive* refers to the motivational strategies implemented in order to keep students on-task; and the *Time* element to instruction is concerned with appropriate pacing of the instruction and how to allocate time to cover all lesson components for example, introduction, revision, new knowledge and engagement activities.

From a constructivist perspective, Merrill (2002) acknowledges the interdependence between instruction and pedagogy and proposed "the First Principles of Instruction" (Merrill, 2002, p. 43). In this model he incorporates five steps or guiding principles. By 'principle' Merrill refers to the critical necessity of acknowledging the relationship between teacher-learners, based in and around learning materials and resources. Merrill (2002) argues these principles are the basis of an instructional design, from which effective and efficient learning can be anticipated. Merrill (2002) proposes authentic learning will occur when:

- "learners are engaged in solving real-world problems" (problem-solving).
- "existing knowledge is activated as a foundation for new knowledge" (using learner's prior knowledge).
- "new knowledge is demonstrated to the learner" (teacher applying knowledge in practice).
- "new knowledge is applied by the learner" (learner receiving opportunity to apply knowledge in practice).

- "new knowledge is integrated into the learner's world" (using learned knowledge in the real world) (Merrill, 2002, pp. 44–45).

Merrill's model reflects a constructivist pedagogical approach transformed into an instructional design. His principles can be implemented in any educational system as they are related to teachers and students co-"creating learning environments and products rather than describing how learners acquire knowledge and skill from these environments or products" (Merrill, 2002, p. 44).

With reference to the research undertaken for this book, examining the EMI lecturers' classroom instruction in terms of these two models of instruction has potential. Both models emphasize student-centered instruction in favour of the more traditional teacher-directed, subject matter-driven instruction where students are confined to being passive recipients of knowledge or information. Both enable an examination of whether the EMI lecturers are positioning students at the centre of the learning supported by instruction that aims to impart the knowledge and skills to solve real world problems. With reference to these models questions arose that have provided a framework for observations and data analysis for this book. These include: Does the EMI lecturers' instruction demonstrate that the information is presented in a way that students can easily follow, for example, in an organized and orderly way, with notable transitions to new topics, clear and simple language, and facilitated with images and examples? Do they attempt to accommodate instruction to the range of the students' levels of prior knowledge and diverse needs? Do they attempt to engage students through various strategies such as using real world problem-based instruction and/or arousing student curiosity through creating intrinsic interest in the material to be taught? Do they allow opportunities for students to discover learning through applying what has been learned into practical, real-life contexts? Do they allow students to share the responsibility for learning time? Finally, do they encourage students to take control of and be accountable for, their own learning during lectures and assessments?

Whilst all three concepts within EMI – the 'English', the 'Medium', and the 'Instruction' are important to gain an understanding of EMI as it is implemented, the importance of 'Instruction' is paramount. It reveals the lecturers' ideologies and pedagogical preferences which in turn reflects the degree of control and power shared between the lecturers and their students ultimately contributing to the success or otherwise of their EMI units and courses.

## 2.5 Conclusion

This Chapter has provided a conceptual understanding of English as a Medium of Instruction. By unpacking the individual words within EMI, it attempts to move beyond the general descriptive accounts of EMI as teaching a subject/course/program in English, with the intention to provide an understanding of what English, Medium and Instruction mean for EMI lecturers' actual teaching and for students' learning. Firstly, the 'English' in EMI is conceptualized from a multilingual theoretical base questioning the notions that EMI is the sole business of monolingual Anglophones. The argument proposed is that there is not one universal English in EMI, but rather 'Englishes' as a Medium of Instruction. The implication is that native English should not be the norm for EMI lecturers to the detriment of translanguaging, which is the nature and reality for many EMI classes. Secondly the conceptualization of 'Medium' is beyond an interpretation that EMI is English as a 'method' of Instruction. 'Medium' is a 'channel' through which teaching is delivered and it is often embedded in or blended with multimedia technology thus can be synchronous and asynchronous. It influences and is influenced by mode, field, tenor and context. Careful consideration and deconstruction of the 'Medium' is necessary to understand EMI lecturers' use of their version of 'English'. Lastly, the 'Instruction' in EMI should not be synonymous with a set of objective rules or principles that can stand universally as those with a positivist perspective would suggest and promote. It is not a mechanical, lock step, linear process akin to experiments conducted in a laboratory. Instead, instruction can be represented as a set of principles based on an individual educators' pedagogical positioning and her/his view of students' needs. Effective instructional design should address students' prior knowledge, their cognitive levels, and enable students to be engaged and motivated in their learning. Based on this conceptualization of EMI, the following Chapters delve into the specific examples and analysis of actual EMI teaching.

# References

Berger, J., & Iyengar, R. (2013). Communication channels and word of mouth: How the medium shapes the message. *Journal of Consumer Research, 40*, 567–579. https://doi.org/10.1086/671345

Biesta, G., & Miedema, S. (2002). Instruction or pedagogy? The need for a transformative conception of education. *Teaching and Teacher Education, 18*, 173–181.

Canagarajah, S. (2011). Translanguaging in the classroom: Emerging issues for research and pedagogy. *Applied Linguistics Review, 2*, 1–28. https://doi.org/10.1515/9783110239331.1

Chafe, W. (1985). Linguistic differences produced by differences between speaking and writing. In D. Olson, N. Torrance, & A. Hildyard (Eds.), *Literacy, language and learning* (pp. 105–124). Cambridge University Press.

Coyle, D. (2007). Content and language integrated learning: Towards a connected research agenda for CLIL pedagogies. *International Journal of Bilingual Education and Bilingualism, 10*(5), 543–562.

Cummins, J. (2001). Bilingual children's mother tongue: Why is it important for education? *Sprogforum, 7*(19), 15–20.

Davies, A. (1996). Proficiency or the native speaker: What are we trying to achieve in ELT? In G. Cook & B. Seidlhofer (Eds.), *Principle and practice in applied linguistics* (pp. 145–159). Oxford University Press.

Dearden, J. (2014). *English as a medium of instruction – A growing global phenomenon; interim report.* University of Oxford.

Douglas Fir Group. (2016). A transdisciplinary framework for SLA in a multilingual world. *The Modern Language Journal, 100*(Supplement, 2016), 19–47.

Eisner, E. (1994). *The educational imagination*. Prentice Hall.
Garcia, O. (2009). *Bilingual education in the 21st century: A global perspective*. Basil/Blackwell.
García, O., & Li, W. (2014). *Translanguaging: Language, bilingualism and education*. Palgrave Macmillan.
Gutierrez, K., Baquedano-Lopez, P., & Alvarez, H. (2001). Literacy as hybridity: Moving beyond bilingualism in urban classrooms. In M. De la Luz Reyes & J. Halcón (Eds.), *The best for our children: Critical perspectives on literacy for Latino students* (pp. 122–141). Teachers College Press.
Halliday, M. A. (1999). The notion of 'context' in language education. In M. Ghadessy (Ed.), *Text and context in funcitonal linguistics* (pp. 1–24). John Benjamins. https://doi.org/10.1075/cilt.169.04hal
Hyun, E. (2006). Transforming instruction into pedagogy through curriculum negotiation. *Journal of Curriculum and Pedagogy, 3*(1), 136–164. https://doi.org/10.1080/15505170.2006.10411587
Jarvis, S., & Pavlenko, A. (2008). *Crosslinguistic influence in language and cognition*. Routledge.
Kachru, B., & Nelson, C. (1996). World Englishes. In S. McKay & N. Hornberger (Eds.), *Sociolinguistics and language teaching* (pp. 71–102). Cambridge University Press.
Kress, G. (2010). *Multimodality: A social semiotic approach to contemporary communication*. Routledge.
Kubota, R. (2013). Language is only a tool: Japanese expatriates working in China and implications for language teaching. *Multilingual Education, 3*(1), 1–20.
Merrill, D. (2002). First principles of instruction. *Educational Technology Research and Development, 50*(3), 43–59. https://doi.org/10.1007/BF02505024
Morais, A. (1999). Is there any change in science educational reforms? A sociological study of theories of instruction. *British Journal of Sociology of Education, 20*(1), 37–53. https://doi.org/10.1080/01425699995489
Murahata, G., Murahata, Y., & Cook. V. (2016). Research questions and methodology of multi-competence. In W. Li & V. Cook (Eds.), *The Cambridge handbook of linguistic multi-competence*. Cambridge University Press. Research questions and methodology of multi-competence. https://doi.org/10.1017/CBO9781107425965.002.
Murray, D. (1988). The context of oral and written language: A framework for mode and medium switching. *Language in Society, 17*, 351–373.
Ringbom, H. (2006). *Cross-linguistic similarity in foreign language learning*. Multilingual Matters.
Roy, S., & Galiev, A. (2011). Discourses on bilingualism in Canadian French immersion programs. *The Canadian Modern Language Review, 67*(3), 351–376. https://doi.org/10.3138/cmlr.67.3.351
Rubin, D. L. (1987). Divergence and convergence between oral and written communication. *Topics in Language Disorders, 7*(4), 1–18. https://doi.org/10.1097/00011363-198709000-00003
Shohamy, E. (2011). Assessing multilingual competencies: Adopting constructive valid assessment policies. *Modern Language Journal, 95*(3), 418–429.
Slavin, R. (1995). A model of effective instruction. *The Educational Forum, 59*(2), 166–176. https://doi.org/10.1080/00131729509336383
Tennyson, R., & Merrill, D. (1971). Hierarchical models in the development of a theory of instruction: A comparison of Bloom, Gagne and Merrill. *Educational Technology, 11*(9), 27–31.
Traugott, C., & Romaine, S. (1985). Some questions for the definition of "style" in socio-historical linguistics. *Folia Linguistica Historica., 6*(1), 7–40. https://doi.org/10.1515/flih.1985.6.1.7
Trimbur, J. (2008). The Dartmouth conference and the geohistory of the native speaker. *College English, 71*(2), 142–169.
Watson, B. (Translator) (1993). *Selected Poems of Su Tung-Po*. Copper Canyon Press.

**Open Access** This chapter is licensed under the terms of the Creative Commons Attribution 4.0 International License (http://creativecommons.org/licenses/by/4.0/), which permits use, sharing, adaptation, distribution and reproduction in any medium or format, as long as you give appropriate credit to the original author(s) and the source, provide a link to the Creative Commons license and indicate if changes were made.

The images or other third party material in this chapter are included in the chapter's Creative Commons license, unless indicated otherwise in a credit line to the material. If material is not included in the chapter's Creative Commons license and your intended use is not permitted by statutory regulation or exceeds the permitted use, you will need to obtain permission directly from the copyright holder.

# Chapter 3
# Chinese Lecturers' Pedagogical Position and Instructional Practice in EMI Teaching

**Abstract** This Chapter reports the pedagogical alignment and instructional practices contributing to the Chinese lecturers' EMI implementation as evidenced in this research data. It counters a predominance in the current literature highlighting EMI research on language with less concern on pedagogy. Evidence of the EMI lecturers' actual classroom instructions and their pedagogical positions were collected and analyzed. Their instruction was identified as being on the continuum between expository and constructivist teaching, with more leaning towards an expository approach in their teaching. The data disclose that the reasons for this prevalence of expository teaching are based on the lecturers' rational choice rather than any overall attribution to their educational culture. Perceiving undergraduate education as the foundational stage of tertiary education and their self-assessment of their role as the main knowledge resource contributed to their distinctive pedagogical view and instructional practices in EMI teaching.

**Keywords** Pedagogy · Instruction · Expository teaching · Constructivist teaching

## 3.1 Introduction

As briefed in the introductory Chapter, the prevalence of English monolingualism in EMI has been extensively studied, however studies concerned with instruction and pedagogy have been reported more marginally. Those studies reporting EMI pedagogy or teaching strategies, do so, primarily at the level of discussion, with suggestions and calls for pedagogical training to improve EMI programs. Some suggested developing thoughtfully designed workshops or structured short courses (Macaro et al., 2018), and others stressed the significance of pedagogical training with a dual focus – language and content (Blosser, 2000; Doiz et al., 2013; Han et al., 2019; Phan, 2021). Additional studies contend pedagogy or instruction as predominantly consisting of language learning (Jiang et al., 2019), and language strategies such as backchannelling (Jawhar, 2012) and codeswitching (Sahan, 2020; Tarnopolsky & Goodman, 2014). Universities as the key stakeholders in EMI programs, are yet to play an important role in EMI pedagogical and instructional development (O'Dowd, 2018; Phan, 2021). A study by O'Dowd (2018) reports the findings of a survey of EMI programs in Europe, concluding that most universities offering a significant number of subjects through EMI, admitted they did not provide pedagogical training or guidance for their EMI lecturers. This lack of leadership on the part of the institutions resulted in lecturers and teachers in the field being left to their own devices for professional learning (PL), which apart from improving their own English, left little or no direction for improving EMI programs (O'Dowd, 2018; Phan, 2021).

Within the literature, two 'successful' EMI pedagogical programs have been reported. Guarda and Helm (2017) reported an EMI professional learning intervention (part of a project called *Learning English for Academic Purpose*) in Italy. Through interview and survey data, the participant lecturers suggested a range of strategies that were addressed in the PL and subsequently considered useful in their teaching. These included student-centered approaches, encouraging moments for students to lead, engaging students through group work, using technology such as video clips to activate students' participation and facilitate lecturers' information transmission. The second report is from Taiwan where a researcher, Chuang (2015) reported one lecturer's 'successful' EMI teaching strategies in an EMI course. This lecturer's strategies included slowing the teaching pace, embedding student activities in class, switching to L1 for key terms and concepts, using simplified English, and incorporating group tasks. These two studies could be considered 'successful' pedagogical research to a degree as both focused on specific teaching strategies and the dedication to include and reflect on students' needs. Whilst claiming to be research investigating pedagogy, these reports highlight a descriptive approach to the strategies of instruction, rather than foregrounding 'pedagogy' and its influence on this instruction.

This review of EMI research studies suggests that EMI and/or Content and Language Integrated Learning (CLIL) pedagogy has plateaued at the level of rich discussion but lacks a body of systematic and in-depth research. Instruction, as a focused research area in EMI, is yet to be rigorously investigated and reported in the literature. This Chapter attempts to address this paucity in the literature by examining the pedagogical approaches of the EMI lecturers' in this research, to investigate how this informed their instructional practice. In order to do so, it is important to examine the lecturers' construction of pedagogy and instruction outside of their EMI teaching as a benchmark from which to reflect on actual EMI teaching episodes. This approach also aims to advance the importance of analyzing evidence-based practice to improve EMI teaching and learning.

## 3.2 Pedagogy and Approaches to Instruction

As a concept, pedagogy has been contested. In this research its definition and purpose is not to address the many forms contributing to its understanding but rather to provide one perspective on pedagogy to assist in the examination in what is termed in this book, EMI pedagogy. Watkins and Mortimore (1999) provide a suitably complex model to conceptualize pedagogy, specifying the relationships between its key elements: the teacher, the classroom or other context, content, the view of learner and learning. Firstly, when considering 'the teacher' questions such as, what is the teachers' role or their view of their role can assist in understanding their pedagogy. For example, whether they act as an 'authoritarian' or democratic agent. Some literature on Western and Asian or Chinese teachers' roles has been found around this polarized division (Biggs, 1996, Biggs & Watkins, 2001; Hofstede, 2011). Secondly, 'the context' as a defining element of pedagogy lays bare the life in the classroom and the complex, dynamic teacher-student interactions, along with the teachers' managerial and organizational aspects in classroom teaching. Thirdly, 'the content' contributes to an understanding of pedagogy as 'how to teach' is often influenced by 'what to teach' which links to teachers' subject knowledges. Finally, notions of 'the learner' take a central position in defining and understanding pedagogy. Views on learners' cognition and motivation directly influence the conceptualization of pedagogy. Watkins and Mortimore (1999) particularly emphasize the learner and contend that educators need to be increasingly conscious of the learner as an active co-constructor of knowledge.

Pedagogy has no absolute certainty and predictability due to these four subjective intermingled dimensions. This conceptualization further confirms that pedagogy cannot be a simple "set of strategies and skills used to teach and test for pre-specified subject matter" (Giroux, 2016, p. 60). It cannot be treated as "fixed principles and practices that can be applied indiscriminately" (Giroux, 2016, p. 65). As the science or art of teaching, it embraces and reflects contextually (social, political and cultural) adjusted practices resulting from negotiations between teachers, learners and the content. Further, Mason (1998) and Morais (1999) claim pedagogic discourse can be identified as being on a continuum between two extremes – the knowledge transmission-oriented expository pedagogy and knowledge development focused constructivist pedagogy. However, it needs to be noted that research has not provided sufficient empirical evidence to attest to the effectiveness of one over the other (Struyven et al., 2010). Constructivism, as a learning theory, holds that learners do not just 'take in' information, but actively engage in constructing their own new knowledge in a sense-making process to engage with the world. It is exemplified in discovery learning classrooms where teachers and learners engage in the co-construction and transformation of knowledge into real-world applications and skills development (Hyun, 2006). Other scholars have similarly identified a continuum of approaches to pedagogy in practice, with a dichotomy of end points. For example, Giroux (2016, p. 60) identifies a similar dichotomy of positions as "conservative and progressive".

Watkins and Mortimore (1999) maintain that pedagogy is the basis from which the teacher or lecturer views their role which then translates into their instruction and their personal teaching style. Therefore, an educator's pedagogical stance should and will necessarily align with and be reflected in their instructional methods. Accordingly, expository pedagogy driven by a positivist learning theory may view knowledge as scientific in nature and transmittable through sequence-based (step locked) instruction. Expository pedagogy may be reflected in teaching styles that designate the role for teachers as dominant and learners as passive, where instruction is subject matter-driven, and focuses on direct teaching of subject facts and truths. Learners receive knowledge as information and are instructed in specific skill development. Alternatively, instruction informed by constructivist pedagogy, will be a learner-driven exercise, and the learners' previous experience and capability will be considered in the planning for learning.

Merrill's (2002) First Principles of Instruction and Salvin's (1995) QAIT Instruction Models outlined in Chap. 2, together with the conceptualization of pedagogy proposed by Watkins and Mortimore's (1999) provides the framework for analyzing the EMI lecturers' data collected throughout this research. Based on the above, a number of questions can be proposed to assist with identifying the pedagogical and instructional position of the EMI lecturers as demonstrated in their teaching. These include: Do the lecturers dominate the class, demonstrating their leaning towards authoritativeness, or do they integrate and engage students in teaching exhibiting a more democratic approach? How does the context, their institution, influence their understanding of an established pedagogy? How do they manage and organize the students and what types of teacher-student interactions are established? What do they know and how do they address their students' cognitive level, for example, prior knowledge and learning styles? The answers to these questions polarize pedagogical orientations, however can assist in understanding what drives actual EMI lecturing practices.

## 3.3 Literature of Pedagogical Positioning and Instructional Practice in China

As the research informing this chapter was conducted in a Chinese university, it needs to be acknowledged that much research reported in the literature on teaching and learning in general, not EMI specifically, has made claims that in Confucius heritage countries, expository pedagogy is the tradition and widely practiced (Biggs, 1996; Biggs & Watkins, 2001; Hofstede, 2011; Lee, 1996; Nguyen et al., 2005; Saravanamuthu, 2008; Tran, 2013; Watkins & Biggs, 2001). More recently, research has reported that China has been influenced by the educational philosophies of the West (Zhao et al., 2016). Constructivism is identified and accepted as a dominant theory in the West and is experiencing a trial from idea to practice in current pedagogical reforms (Tan, 2017). However, research reporting examples of expository teaching abound. For example, the study by Zhao et al. (2016) analyzed classroom observations across three high schools and found an expository approach was dominant, being identified in 16 of the 27 lessons observed, with only two lessons being taught through a constructivist, inquiry and transformative approach. Yan (2015) investigated a group of high school teachers' responses to a reform of English curriculum and noted a considerable mismatch between the teachers' perceptions of the new curriculum and their classroom practices. The data revealed that the methods of instruction were teacher-centred, textbook-based and test-driven despite advanced pedagogies introduced in the new curriculum. This resonates with the previous research mentioned above. The findings also acknowledged the challenges for teachers and lecturers to adopt a constructivist pedagogical approach in the current educational context in China. These included critiques by teachers that constructivism undermined content mastery, was incompatible with the traditional knowledge-transmission approach, and was misaligned with the prevailing assessment system in China (Tan, 2017). These studies indicate that without changing the examination-oriented system and increasing teacher's agency and autonomy, constructivist teaching will not be achieved (Yan, 2015).

Using one university as the case, this research sought to investigate: What are the prevailing instructional methods implemented by EMI lecturers? and Will these lecturers implement expository teaching and topic-based instruction unanimously as predicated by previous research studies? Therefore, the pedagogical position and instructional practices of the EMI lecturers in this research are central in this Chapter. In addition to the questions posed above, this Chapter also aims to answer: What are the identifiable features of these Chinese EMI lecturers' instructional practice? and How does their instruction reflect their pedagogy?

### 3.3.1 The EMI Lecturers' Perception of Teaching and Learning

To gauge the EMI lecturers' pedagogical positioning a survey was administered (N = 69) which sought to collect the lecturers' responses to questions on lecturer-student reciprocity in their interactions, their understanding of learning and knowledge, their control of the content and the role of students' knowledge. The statements (Table 3.1) were listed in pairs with the left statement denoting an Expository position, whilst the statement on the right was couched in Constructivist terms. The participants were asked to tick the box next to the statement that best represented their view. Alternatively, a third choice was offered – Balance of the Two if both statements in the same row were considered equally true or should be combined. The final row of the end of the survey allowed participants to provide any additional information. The raw data tallies, and overall percentages are displayed in the table below.

**Table 3.1** EMI lecturers' pedagogical standing (Survey data)

| | Expository | | Balance of the Two | Constructivist | |
|---|---|---|---|---|---|
| Teacher & students' role | Teacher should be given the authority | 26 | 32 | 11 | Students should be given the democracy. |
| | Teacher is knowledge holder | 29 | 29 | 11 | Students are co-constructor of meaning. |
| | Teacher should cover the teaching. | 19 | 34 | 16 | Students themselves should be given time to explore their learning in class. |
| Context and classroom dynamics | Teacher should dominate class time. | 41 | 20 | 8 | Students should dominate the class time. |
| | Learning should occur through teacher's presentation | 19 | 36 | 14 | Learning should occur through interaction and activities. |
| | Lecturer should focus on individual learning. | 48 | 18 | 3 | Lecturers should create opportunities for students to learn from each other. |
| Control of the content | Textbook should be the only resource in teaching. | 17 | 30 | 22 | Multiple other resources should be equally included in teaching. |
| | Learning should be arranged topic by topic following text. | 39 | 19 | 11 | Learning should focus on problem solving. |
| | Assessment should focus on checking textbook knowledge. | 34 | 18 | 17 | Assessment should focus on checking problem solving and critical thinking. |
| Understanding of learning and knowledge | Learning factual knowledge and information should be the focus. | 17 | 40 | 12 | Content understanding and conceptual development should be the focus. |
| | Learning should focus on cognitive development. | 30 | 33 | 6 | Learning should focus on meta-cognitive development. |
| | Learning should focus on knowledge retention. | 19 | 38 | 12 | Learning should focus on solving real problems. |
| | | 338 = 40.8% | 347 = 41.9% | 143 = 17.3% | |
| Comments and clarifications (e.g. general pedagogical issues)[a] | Please include here any comment or clarification | | | | |

[a]Note: Data from comments are presented in a following section

The survey data reveal that the number and relative percentage of responses supporting each category was: Expository Statements N = 338 (40.8%), Constructivist Statements N = 143 (17.3%), and the number for agreeing to a Balance of the Two N = 347 (41.9%). It can be argued from these results, that a purely constructivist pedagogical position is held by very few of these Chinese EMI lecturers. Most responses were recorded in the middle ground category, arguably the safe space, however, only slightly less were those consistently predisposed to statements revealing an expository pedagogy.

On closer examination, the individual statements, 12 in all, revealed differences of opinion across the four survey themes. Within the scores for statements considering 'lecturers and students' roles', a large number of the lecturers were willing to consider the balance between sharing the authority in the classroom with their students (32/69) in order to allow students some space to explore their learning. However, a considerable number of EMI lecturer's (29/69) believe the teacher should maintain the position of power in their classes. In terms of the 'context and classroom dynamics', more than half of the lecturers (36/69) agree that lectures should be based on the lecturers' presentation integrated with interaction and students' activities. On the other hand, the majority recorded scores that lecturers should control the class time (41/69) and should focus on individual learning rather than create opportunities for teamwork (48/69). The responses from this category indicate the predisposition of these EMI lecturers to teach within a one-way teacher-centered classroom environment – expository pedagogy.

Regarding the lecture 'content' statements, nearly half of the participants (30/69) believe multiple resources (textbooks and other resources) should be drawn upon in teaching. When viewing teaching content and assessment, many lecturers (39/69) were less flexible, believing subject matter should be systematically covered topic by topic according to a textbook. When considering 'assessment' processes, half the respondents supported knowledge checking in the textbook (34/69), a quarter believe that assessment should focus on problem solving and critical thinking (17/69), and the last quarter revealed the view that assessment should include both approaches (18/69). With the statements investigating responses to an 'understanding of learning itself', the middle ground option (combining both the statements for constructivist and also expository pedagogy), was the most prominent response across all three statements. The only statement where the expository view almost equalled the combination of both, was that learning should focus on cognitive development (30/69), whereas the majority thought meta-cognition and cognition were both important (33/69). With the remaining two statements the majority view was clearly that learning should be a combination of factual knowledge acquisition and conceptual development (40/69), and that knowledge retention and real-life problem solving (38/69) were most important.

## 3.3.2 EMI Lecturers' Additional Comments

The qualitative data gathered in the commentary box at the conclusion of the survey provided a voice for the EMI lecturers to justify their responses and to flag issues that were important to them. These commentaries provided additional details for their survey responses thus enabling a deeper understanding of their pedagogical position. Data indicate that the lecturers' pedagogical view is situated within their convictions around the foundational nature of undergraduate education, institutional expectation to achieve learning outcomes, and students' predisposition towards an expectation of the learning environment provided at university level. A snapshot of comments is presented below as representative of EMI lecturers' opinions (EMI lecturers have been de-identified as E, X, Y, Z).

> Making the students at the center of the classroom is all so ideal. Practically they rely on the teacher's explanation so much for content knowledge. The teacher's explanation is still the most efficient way to make them understand the subject knowledge in the minimum timeline (Lecturer X).

> Students' self-learning ability is so weak. If you give them a task to work out between them, they won't go too far. Most were previously not trained to work or solve a problem in a team. The learning habit was inherited from their high school and even primary schooling. They are so comfortable to be fed information most of the time. (Lecturer Z).

> Classroom time is so short and so valuable. Letting students play in class would be primary school's business. Students feel that I waste their time if I don't teach but let them work between themselves. I ask them to work on the exercises after class. They are in class to listen to me because I believe I have a lot to offer (Lecturer E).

> I would allow more discussion or self-exploration for my postgraduate students. They are undergraduate. I need to cover the whole book topic by topic. They need solid and consistent knowledge in the textbook. To pass this subject and to eventually graduate, they need to have this foundational knowledge before they do anything else (Lecturer Y).

A lecturers' role in any university is to fulfill the mission of their institution and teach students successfully towards graduation. The identity of a lecturer and the development of his/her pedagogical position is shaped within this context as the data excerpts above demonstrate.

Lecturer Z reiterates the view that the students themselves are not independent learners as progressing through an education system based on 'teacher-as-the-sage' classroom practices, they are "so comfortable to be fed [information] most of the time". This lecturer contends that students have inherited a dependency on the teacher as knowledge provider from their early stages of schooling – primary and secondary. Although other lecturers recorded that encouraging students' own exploration in their learning was preferred, it was a finding that lecturers saw the students' expectation of a certain method of instruction as informing their practice.

Whilst the point was made that students at university expect the same type of instruction as they experienced previously in their primary and secondary schooling, Lecturer Y made a distinction between undergraduate and postgraduate education. This lecturer commented that within a postgraduate or research degree study there were possibilities to encourage 'discussion or self-exploration', however in the undergraduate space the focus needed to be the accumulation of subject knowledge. Lecturer Y's view is supported by the institutional expectation for students to achieve the listed 'graduate attributes' before they complete their degrees.

Another theme identified across comments provided by the lecturers was that of time efficiency and trust (Lecturers X, Y, Z, E). The students, according to these lecturers, and the lecturers themselves have an expectation and trust in the expert knowledge they will impart in a systematic and efficient way (E). By efficient, there is the belief that class time is short and valuable; students exploring their own learning is more time consuming (E). This foregrounding of trust and efficiency assigns the lecturers into a position of leading the responsibility for students' learning. Comments such as 'play in class' (E), 'waste of time' (E), 'foundational knowledge first' (Y); 'teacher's explanation is the most efficient', 'students at the center is so ideal' (X) indicate expository pedagogy is central for these participant EMI lecturers.

### 3.3.3  *The Design Features of EMI Lecturers' Instruction*

The data collected in this section of the research was gathered through direct observations of the actual classroom teaching of 19 EMI lecturers. The researcher was present in the classroom (a space accommodating 60–80 students) as an observer and note taker throughout the 90 min of the scheduled lecture for all 19 lectures. The observational data were then collated and reported as findings from the participating EMI lecturers as a group. Individual differences in EMI lecturer's designs and features of their instruction was not the focus. The concern was to map the 'volume' or the trend in the observational data against Merrill's (2002) Principles of Instruction which are couched in a constructivist pedagogical vein. As the researcher observed the teaching, the number of times an episode within the lesson reflected one of the five principles, a tally mark was made in the relevant column against that principle. In this way it could be identified how closely the EMI lecturers' instructional features aligned with constructivist pedagogy.

Data revealed the majority of EMI lecturers were implementing instruction reflective of an expository pedagogy as outlined in Table 3.2.

### 3.3.4  *Topic-Based Versus Problem-Centered Instruction*

The first principle of Merrill's (2002, p. 45) instructional model is whether the instruction is topic-based or problem-centered which answers the critical question: Are learners engaged in finding solutions to real-world problems? Similarly, in

**Table 3.2** Observation of EMI lecturers' instruction

| Classes observed N = 19 (90 min/lesson) | 1. Problem raised | 2. Engaging prior knowledge (# times) | 3. New knowledge presented by lecturers with examples and/or practical explanation (minutes) | 4. Activities for learners to apply learning (minutes) | 5. Activities for real world problem solving |
|---|---|---|---|---|---|
| Engineering | No | Yes, 5–10 | >60 Yes | <15 | No |
| Engineering | No | Yes, <5 | >60 Yes | <15 | No |
| Engineering | No | Yes, 5–10 | >60 Yes | <15 | No |
| Computer science | No | Yes, <5 | >60 Yes | <15 | No |
| Computer science | No | Yes, 5–10 | >60 No | <15 | No |
| Computer science | No | Yes, <5 | >60 Yes | <15 | No |
| Computer science | No | Yes, <5 | >60 Yes | <15 | No |
| Computer science | No | Yes, <5 | >60 Yes | <15 | No |
| Finance | No | No | >60 No | <15 | No |
| Biology | Yes | Yes, >10 | 30–60 Yes | >30 | Yes |
| Biology | No | Yes, 5–10 | >60 Yes | <15 | No |
| Medical science | Yes | Yes, >10 | 30–60 Yes | >30 | Yes |
| Maths | No | Yes, >10 | >60 No | <15 | No |
| Physics | No | Yes, 5–10 | >60 No | <15 | No |
| Biochemistry | Yes | Yes, 5–10 | 30–60 Yes | >30 | Yes |
| Philosophy | Yes | Yes, 5–10 | <30 No | >60 | No |
| French | No | Yes, >10 | 30–60 Yes | >30 | No |
| International relationship | Yes | Yes, >10 | 30–60 Yes | >30 | No |
| Physical education | Yes | Yes, >10 | 30–60 Yes | >30 | Yes |

Adapted from Merrill's First Principles of Instruction (2002, pp. 44–45)

Slavin's (1995) QAIT model, the term 'incentive' is used to address the degree to which the teacher should engage and motivate the learners to work on instructional tasks. The observational data reveal that one third of the lecturers (6/19) posed problems and explored solutions as central to their lectures. They tended to emphasize an holistic task as the focus for the entire lesson. Learning objectives were specifically outlined to students at the beginning, with clear teaching plans designed to achieve these objectives. Student participation was predominantly their prepared presentations. The remaining two thirds (13/19) of the lecturers were observed implementing topic-centered instruction. In these classes, a lesson commenced with an introduction to the teaching topic, and after presenting new knowledge or information, concluded with a component of demonstration. There were limited observable activities or interactions organized as the instruction was overwhelmingly teacher talk. Teaching components were in isolation rather than related to a task to complete or a problem to solve. As recorded in Table 3.2 above, the fields of study with a 'No' response in column 1, were dominantly the STEM fields (Science Technology Engineering and Mathematics) whereas the teaching in the Social Sciences fields demonstrated a problem-centered approach. Overall, the co-existence of the two modes of instruction exemplifies the division in this group's pedagogical position, with the majority reflecting an expository pedagogy.

### 3.3.5 Instruction Linking Prior and New Knowledge

The second principle of Merrill's (2002) model applied in this data collection and analysis translates to: Do lecturers purposively activate learners' "relevant previous experience" (p. 45) as the basis for connecting with new knowledge? Similarly, with the QAIT Model of Instruction (Slavin, 1995) the connection between new content and students' background knowledge is emphasized. The observational data in this research revealed that during their teaching, 18/19 lecturers directed students to recollect some previously taught and learned knowledge. The lecturers were noted moving back and forth between an explanation of new knowledge and requiring students to recall the information from previous lessons however the number of times this principle was implemented varied. The numerical data were then collapsed into three categories of frequency with reference to links to pre-existing knowledge: more than 10 times; between 5 and 10; and less than 5 times (including 0).

An analysis of these data revealed one third of the lecturers explicitly linked students' existing and new knowledge, more than 10 times during the 90 min of class time. Another third emphasized the links between prior and new knowledge 5–10 times and an additional six lecturers (one third) very rarely used this principle of instruction (0–5 times) (see Table 3.2: Column 2). As 18/19 lecturers initiated this principle of instruction to some degree, no matter what pedagogical position the lecturers held, there was recognition that this principle was important. We could extrapolate from the frequency with which this principle was used, that those lecturers connecting prior and new knowledge over ten times during a lesson, are explicitly using this approach as it reflects their constructivist pedagogy. Likewise, those lecturers moving the new knowledge forward in isolation or with a quick review of the content of the previous lesson, are displaying a commitment to an expository pedagogy. The data show the number of lecturers in each category as being almost equal in numbers 6/19 and 7/19. Those in the middle category are not overly committed to activating prior knowledge as the foundation for new knowledge but given the frequency of use is 5–10 times, realize it has merit.

## 3.3.6 Teacher Talk and Knowledge Demonstration/Explanation by the Lecturer

Merrill's (2002, p.45) third instructional principle is demonstrating new knowledge to the learner. In Slavin's (1995) QAIT (Quality, Appropriateness, Incentive, Time) Model, quality instruction is specified as needing to have information presented through clear and simple language, so lessons are easy to follow, and often accompanied with images and examples and facilitated with transitional language between topics. The significance lecturers placed on instruction such as 'remember-what-you-were-told' or 'here are examples, and this is how this new knowledge can be applied' was revealed in the observational data. 60% of the lecturers dominated the talk for more than two thirds (60 min) of the class time, and whilst 30% of lecturers spoke for a lesser amount of time, the total was still in the 30–60 min range (see Table 3.2: Column 3). Outliers to these data were two lecturers who operated flipped classrooms, having the class time dominated by students, who on the particular day of observation, occupied the lecture time with their individual presentations.

In terms of how new knowledge was presented to the students most lecturers structured their teaching by commencing with the new knowledge, theories or concepts, with some subject fields including formulae or rules, followed by further explanations using reasoning and/or examples to illustrate the new knowledge. Data have recorded, not only the time spent in teacher talk, but also whether the lecturer did or did not demonstrate the new knowledge through examples and explanations. Data across the two variables in this principle are presented in Fig. (3.1).

The observation data reveal that five lecturers (5/19–26%) did not include any demonstration for students to support their learning of the new knowledge (combined orange bars). The graph above shows that four of these lecturers were also in the group occupying the most teacher talk (over 60 min) across the 90-min lecture. Their lectures were observed as being structured around PowerPoint slides with little 'unfolding' illustrations, examples or explanations. This resulted in content that was abstract and isolated. These four lecturers were conveying the message to students analogous with 'you need to remember this now and you will understand it later'. It was also observed that these four lecturers were conscious of their English expression which appeared to be an obvious barrier in their teaching. This is the group arguably holding an expository pedagogy as evidence indicates the teacher is the center of knowledge distribution, with little space for student participation and no accounting for the need to explain or provide workable examples to support the learning of all students.

The lecturers observed making concerted efforts to demonstrate new knowledge were 14 in number (14/19–73.5%) (combined blue bars). Of these it is argued that those who spent less time on teacher talk (6/19–31%) would be those reflecting a constructivist pedagogy, with the other 8 lecturers whose talk dominated the lecture time, but yet included demonstrations of the new knowledge, would be on the continuum between expository and constructivist (42%).

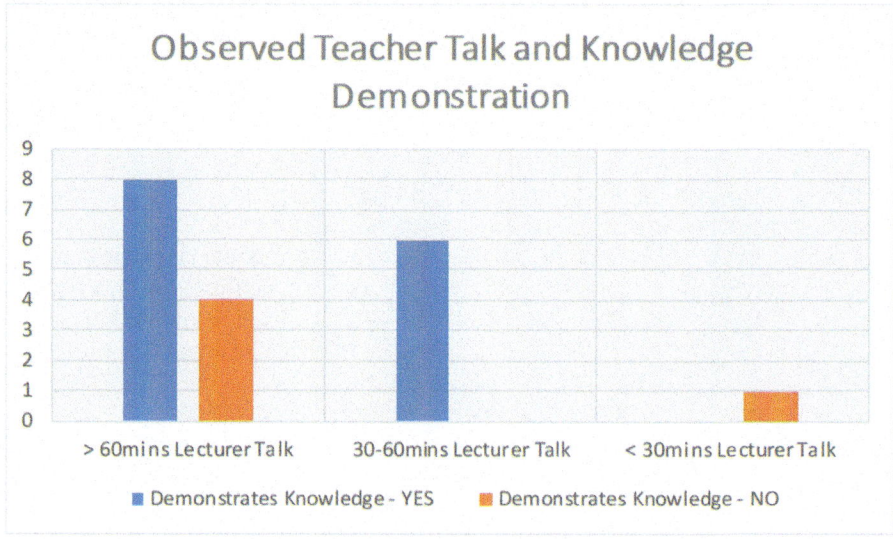

**Fig. 3.1** Teacher talk and knowledge demonstration

### 3.3.7 New Knowledge Application and Integration by the Students in the Real World

Merrill's fourth and fifth instructional principles emphasize opportunities and guidance for learners "to use their new knowledge or skill to solve problems" and "to integrate [transfer] the new knowledge or skill into their everyday life" (Merrill, 2002, p. 46). These two principles shift the responsibility for learning from lecturers to students. From a slightly different angle, Slavin (1995) used the concept of time to measure instruction. That is, how to distribute engagement time for students to apply the learned knowledge in practice.

From the data, the amount of time allocated to student application and integration of knowledge ranged from a maximum of 15 min, more than 30 min and greater than 60 min (which was an outlier). In these practice and application sessions it was also observed as to whether the activities were related to real-life situations or more abstract practice examples. The graph below indicates the results (Fig. 3.2).

The frequency data show in 12 out of the 19 classes observed, students' activities were limited to a maxiumum of 15 min within a 90-min lecture (16% of lecture time). In 7 classes students were actively engaged in upward of 15 min, above 30 min and in one instance over 60 min.

Within the lectures where 15 min or less was allocated to student-focused time, the content was observed to be 'digesting' and 'reflecting' on what the lecturer had presented, basically a question and answer opportunity for clarification. There were fewer activities providing opportunities for group work and/or discussion. The

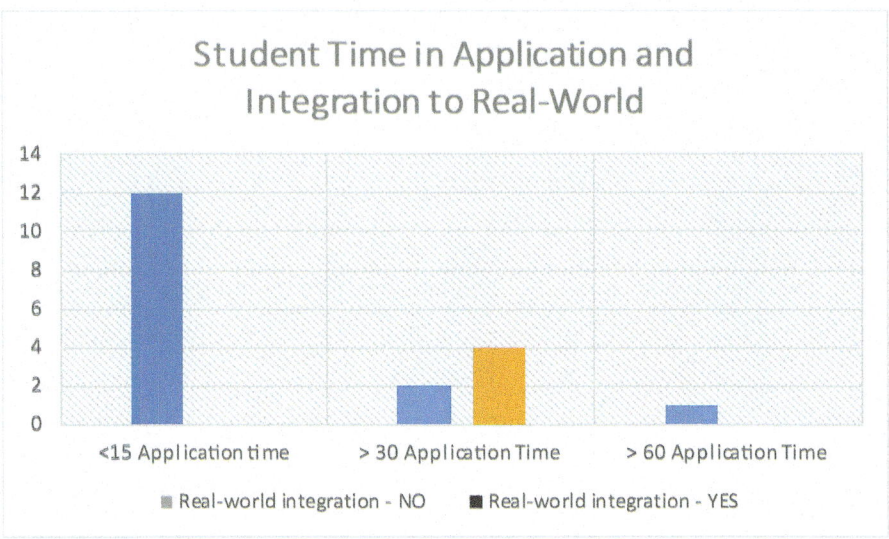

**Fig. 3.2** Student time in knowledge application into the real-world

focus was on direct understanding and/or memorization of the new knowledge rather than application or problem solving.

For those classes where more than 30 min of lecture time was apportioned to students, including the two flipped classes, students were not empowered to apply the learned knowedge in new contexts or to solve real-world problems. Instead, they presented or practiced their understanding of the learned knowledge, theories, concepts, and/or formula. A phenomenon oberved was that during allocated student-based or practice time, students were not working collaboratively with peers. The planned activities required students to work indivdually.

In summary, the survey data indicate, each statement revealing a constructivist pedagogical tone received less than 20% of lecturers' scores. An average of 40% of lecturers agreed with statements reflecting an expository mindset with a further 40% opting for a position somewhere between the two. The observation data reveal the co-existence of topic-based and problem-centered instruction modes which indicates the lecturers varied in their pedagogical positioning. However there was a tendency towards topic-centered instruction as this was implemented by at least two thirds of the lecturers. The majority of the lecturers focused on presenting information and demonstration following the textbook. The application of the learned knowledge in practice and solving real life problems was absent in the practice of all but four lecturers. A final observation was that students' activities were all at an individual level with no group work observed.

## 3.4 The Chinese Lecturers' Pedagogical and Instructional Choice – Cultural or Rational?

From the analysis of the survey and observational data mapped against Merrill's (2002) five key principles of instruction, the finding is that more lecturers hold an expository pedagogical view reflected in their instructional practice, compared to the number of advocates for a constructivist pedagogy and those who attest to an integrated, middle ground approach.

Previous research has explained this phenomenon in terms of cultural determinism, by arguing that culture is the prevailing reason for the prevalence of particular pedagogical views. For example, Biggs (1996), Carroll and Ryan (2005), Merriam and Associates (2007) and Nguyen et al. (2006) contend that in Confucius heritage countries such as China, teachers/lecturers unanimously embrace a teacher-centered pedagogy. These researchers allocate a kind of 'mysticism' to culture as having an all-encompassing effect on pedagogy. Nguyen et al. (2006. p. 1) substantiate this argument further outlining that educational approaches are socially and culturally constrained, with any attempts to adopt educational theories and practices from outside that context, without considering learners' cultural heritage and/or making rigorous adaptations, will be destined to failure. Other researchers, such as Saravanamuthu (2008) and Tran (2013) claim that rather than being purely determined by culture, pedagogy is situated in, and contingent upon, the specific learning requirements reflecting the institution's mission statements on teaching objectives and student learning outcomes.

The premise from the literature cited above is that the EMI lecturers in this study, from the same institution and within a 'Confucius Heritage Culture' could be expected to all hold a similar pedagogical view and instructional practice. This was not the case as the data show their pedagogical views and instructional practices were diverse. The inference from these data is that cultural rationalism is at play. This rationalism can be seen through the lecturers' views, of themselves and their students, around subject knowledge, teaching and learning.

## 3.5 Lecturers' Discipline Knowledge and Teaching

The data indicate that most lecturers believe undergraduate study, as opposed to post-graduate and PhD research training, is foundational education. The majority of the lecturers viewed their role as the primary source of knowledge, their expertise reflected by their qualifications at PhD level and years of experience in their fields. These lecturers would agree with the work of Fernando and Marikar (2017, p. 111) who state a lecturer "possesses more knowledge about the subject he/she is teaching than the average student" and in order to impart this knowledge "teaching must involve transmission of expert knowledge from the teacher to the student". In this study, directing students' learning systematically assisted by textbooks was important to the EMI lecturers especially in the fields of engineering, computer science and mathematics. Observational data in STEM classes revealed teaching episodes dominated by topic-based instruction whereas the teaching in the social sciences, philosophy and international studies, a problem-centered approach was more frequent. Each of the fields lends itself to a different paradigm in teaching and learning.

Fernando and Marikar (2017, p. 111) also argue that "teaching involves both the transmission of knowledge and the facilitation of learning". The majority of these lecturers enacted instruction emphasizing knowledge demonstration/acquisition. Knowledge application in practice and real-world problem-solving contexts were far less frequent. However, the 'facilitation of learning' around cognitive outcomes, was not an aim of this research. It does need to be acknowledged that a quiet, seemingly 'passive' class should not be confused with a lack of cognitive engagement or active thinking on the part of students.

## 3.6 Learners–Passive in Behavior but Active in Thinking

According to the stimulated recall interview data some lecturers in this study, recounted that their students' view of pedagogy and instruction aligned with their own. The lecturers felt comfortable in the belief that their students expected and trusted them to lead the learning and share their expertise in the content knowledge – the most time efficient method of instruction. This view is captured in the quote: "Students feel that I waste their time if I don't teach but let them work between themselves." Thirty-five years ago, a Hong Kong based research study also reported that tertiary students preferred this mode of learning, not because they were incapable, but were demonstrating a rational preference, that is, they would learn more quickly rather than investing their own time in exploring and negotiating the content knowledge when the outcome may not be assured (Biggs, 1996). This research did not engage with students' views, so no claims are made, other than learning styles between students vary and some may prefer to study in a teacher-centered class/lecture room, as described by some lecturers in this study.

Chinese students are often described as passive and rote learners. However, data in this study indicate that most of the lecturers made concerted efforts (18/19) to connect students' prior knowledge, with the new learning to engage learners' cognition. The quiet students may not necessarily be passive and are actually engaging in understanding as well as memorization when processing the new knowledge. Literature supports this argument as Chinese students' academic performance tend to outperform Western students (Saravanamuthu, 2008, p. 152). This result could not be achieved if all learning was rote without understanding and application. Similarly, if the Chinese education system follows Confucianism, then we should expect that Chinese students' learning is intertwined with active thinking. This learning principle is recorded in the Analects II.15 as "seeking knowledge without thinking is labour lost; thinking without seeking knowledge is perilous" (Lee, 1996,

p. 34). Students' quietness should not be confused with passiveness, nor memorization with rote learning as both may equally be demonstrating active thinking and understanding (Tran, 2013).

## 3.7 Conclusion

This research found that EMI lecturers' pedagogical positioning and subsequent teaching practices were based on rational decisions such as teaching in the most efficient way in terms of time and subject matter to cover, and who has more expertise in the subject knowledge – lecturers or students. An overriding claim that culture is the sole determinate of pedagogy and instruction is not supported by the findings in this research. Culture as a monolithic entity, cannot explain the variety or range of pedagogical views and instructional practices observed in this research. Some have argued that economic and social, as well as cultural contexts impact on the development of a teacher's pedagogy. In this research, agreement between a lecturer's understanding of knowledge and learning, and how s/he perceived students' expectations and cognition contributed to the rationality behind their decision making around pedagogical positioning and instructional practice.

With the liberal subjects such as the social sciences, humanities and education, elements of constructivism such as negotiating the curriculum and sharing the leadership in learning is feasible and was observed in these EMI lecturers' teaching. In contrast, in the 'hard' disciplines such as engineering and mathematics, a learning environment couched in constructivism including hands-on activities, collaboration between students and a more informal lecturer-student relationship was not observed in these EMI lecturer's classrooms.

## References

Biggs, J. (1996). Western misperceptions of the Confucian heritage learning culture. In D. Watkins & J. Biggs (Eds.), *The Chinese learner: Cultural, psychological, and contextual influences* (pp. 46–67). Comparative Education Research Centre/Australian Council for Educational Research.

Biggs, J., & Watkins, D. (2001). Insights into teaching the Chinese learner. In D. Watkins & J. Biggs (Eds.), *Teaching the Chinese learner: Psychological and pedagogical perspectives* (pp. 277–300). Comparative Education Research Centre/Australian Council for Educational Research.

Blosser, P. (2000). *How to ask the right questions*. National Science Teachers Association.

Carroll, J., & Ryan, J. (Eds.). (2005). *Teaching international students: Improving learning for all*. Routledge.

Chuang, Y. (2015). An EMI pedagogy that facilitates students' learning. *English Language Teaching, 8*(12), 63–73.

Doiz, A., Lasagabaster, D., & Sierra, J. (Eds.). (2013). *English-medium instruction at universities*. Multilingual Matters.

Fernando, S., & Marikar, F. (2017). Constructivist teaching/learning theory and participatory teaching methods. *Journal of Curriculum and Teaching, 6*(1), 110–122.

Giroux, H. (2016). Beyond pedagogies of repression. *Monthly Review, 67*(10), 57–71.

Guarda, M., & Helm, F. (2017). I have discovered new teaching pathways: The link between language shift and teaching practice. *International Journal of Bilingual Education and Bilingualism, 20*(7), 897–913. https://doi.org/10.1080/13670050.2015.1125848

Han, J., Han, Y., & Ji, X. (2019). Cultural concepts as powerful theoretical tools. Chinese teachers' perceptions of their relationship with students in cross-cultural contexts. *International Journal for the Scholarship of Teaching and Learning, 13*(1). https://doi.org/10.20429/ijsotl.2019.130108

Hofstede, G. (2011). *Dimensionalizing cultures: The Hofstede Model in context. Online readings in psychology and culture, unit 2.* http://scholarworks.gvsu.edu/orpc/vol2/iss1/8.

Hyun, E. (2006). Transforming instruction into pedagogy through curriculum negotiation. *Journal of Curriculum and Pedagogy, 3*(1), 136–164. https://doi.org/10.1080/15505170.2006.10411587

Jawhar, S. (2012). *Conceptualising CLIL in a Saudi context: A corpus linguistic and conversation analytic perspective* (Doctoral dissertation). University of Newcastle Upon Tyne. https://theses.ncl.ac.uk/dspace/bitstream/10443/1849/1/Jawhar12.pdf.

Jiang, L., Zhang, L., & May, S. (2019). Implementing English-medium instruction (EMI) in China: Teachers' practices and perceptions, and students' learning motivation and needs. *International Journal of Bilingual Education and Bilingualism, 22*(2), 107–119.

Lee, W. (1996). The cultural context for Chinese learners: Conceptions of learning in the Confucian tradition. In D. Watkins & J. Biggs (Eds.), *The paradox of the Chinese learner and beyond. Teaching the Chinese learner: Psychological and pedagogical perspectives* (pp. 25–41). Comparative Education Research Centre/Australian Council for Educational Research.

Macaro, E., Curle, S., Pun, J., An, J., & Dearden, J. (2018). A systematic review of English medium instruction in higher education. *Language Teaching, 51*(1), 36–76. https://doi.org/10.1017/S0261444817000350

Mason, L. (1998). Sharing cognition to construct scientific knowledge in school context: The role of oral and written discourse. *Instructional Science, 26*, 359–389.

Merriam, S., & Associates. (2007). *Non-Western perspectives on learning and knowing.* Kreiger Publishing Company.

Merrill, D. (2002). First principles of instruction. *Educational Technology Research and Development, 50*(3), 43–59. https://doi.org/10.1007/BF02505024

Morais, A. (1999). Is there any change in science educational reforms? A sociological study of theories of instruction. *British Journal of Sociology of Education, 20*(1), 37–53. https://doi.org/10.1080/01425699995489

Nguyen, P., Terlouw, C., & Pilot, A. (2005). Cooperative learning vs Confucian heritage culture's collectivism: Confrontation to reveal some cultural conflicts and mismatch. *Asia Europe Journal, 3*, 403–419.

Nguyen, P., Terlouw, C., & Pilot, A. (2006). Culturally appropriate pedagogy: The case of group learning in a Confucian heritage culture context. *Intercultural Education, 17*(1), 1–19.

O'Dowd, R. (2018). The training and accreditation of teachers for English medium instruction: An overview of practice in European universities. *International Journal of Bilingual Education and Bilingualism, 21*, 553–563.

Phan, T. (2021). *Content and Language Integrated Learning: A Case Study of Lecturers' Experiences of Professional Learning for Engineering and English Integrated Learning Program within Vietnamese Higher Education.* A thesis submitted in fulfillment of the requirements for the degree of Doctor of Philosophy, Western Sydney University.

Sahan, K. (2020). ELF interactions in English-medium engineering classrooms. *ELT Journal, 74*(4), 418–427.

Saravanamuthu, K. (2008). Reflecting on the Biggs–Watkins theory of the Chinese learner. *Critical Perspectives on Accounting, 19*, 138–180.

# References

Slavin, R. (1995). A model of effective instruction. *The Educational Forum, 59*(2), 166–176. https://doi.org/10.1080/00131729509336383

Struyven, K., Dochy, F., & Janssens, S. (2010). Teach as you preach: The effects of student-Centred versus lecture-based teaching on student teachers' approaches to teaching. *European Journal of Teacher Education, 33*(1), 43–64.

Tan, C. (2017). Constructivism and pedagogical reform in China: Issues and challenges. *Globalisation, Societies and Education, 15*(2), 238–247. https://doi.org/10.1080/14767724.2015.1105737

Tarnopolsky, O., & Goodman, B. (2014). The ecology of language in classrooms at a university in eastern Ukraine. *Language and Education, 28*(4), 383–396. https://doi.org/10.1080/09500782.2014.890215

Tran, T. (2013). Is the learning approach of students from the Confucian heritage culture problematic? *Education Research for Policy and Practice, 12*, 57–65.

Watkins, D., & Biggs, J. (Eds.). (2001). *The paradox of the Chinese learner and beyond. Teaching the Chinese learner: Psychological and pedagogical perspectives*. Comparative Education Research Centre/Australian Council for Educational Research.

Watkins, C., & Mortimore, P. (1999). Pedagogy: What do we know? In P. Mortimore (Ed.), *Understanding pedagogy and it impact on learning* (pp. 1–19). Paul Chapman Publishing Ltd.

Yan, C. (2015). 'We can't change much unless the exams change': Teachers' dilemmas in the curriculum reform in China. *Improving Schools, 18*(1), 5–19.

Zhao, M., Mu, B., & Lu, C. (2016). Teaching to the test: Approaches to teaching in senior secondary schools in the context of curriculum reform in China. *Creative Education, 7*, 32–43. https://doi.org/10.4236/ce.2016.71004

**Open Access** This chapter is licensed under the terms of the Creative Commons Attribution 4.0 International License (http://creativecommons.org/licenses/by/4.0/), which permits use, sharing, adaptation, distribution and reproduction in any medium or format, as long as you give appropriate credit to the original author(s) and the source, provide a link to the Creative Commons license and indicate if changes were made.

The images or other third party material in this chapter are included in the chapter's Creative Commons license, unless indicated otherwise in a credit line to the material. If material is not included in the chapter's Creative Commons license and your intended use is not permitted by statutory regulation or exceeds the permitted use, you will need to obtain permission directly from the copyright holder.

# Chapter 4
# Chinese EMI Lecturers' Engagement Strategies

**Abstract** In Chap. 3, the pedagogical positions and instructional practices of the EMI lecturers were analyzed. This Chapter continues the examination of actual teaching practice in EMI classes by focusing on the Chinese EMI lecturers' specific engagement strategies. Examining engagement allows this research to respond to two concerns raised in current literature: (i) that expository pedagogy and its aligned instruction will generate less classroom engagement compared to constructivist teaching; and (ii) there is less engagement and interaction in a class when teaching is conducted in EMI. The aim of this Chapter is not to measure the effectiveness of learning in relation to engagement, but rather to capture the characteristics of the engagement strategies implemented by the participants. Data reveal a general pattern in the EMI lecturers' implementation of engagement strategies: cognitive engagement was the dominant, most frequently used engagement strategy, and conversely, emotional, managerial and behavioral engagement was observed with very limited frequency. The arguments being proposed are that the characteristics of these Chinese EMI lecturers' engagement strategies are shaped by their pedagogical, educational and cultural ideologies; and that English as the medium plays a secondary role in patterns of engagement observed in this research.

**Keywords** Engagement · Cognitive engagement · Emotional engagement · Behavioral engagement · Managerial engagement

## 4.1 Introduction – Does the Choice of Pedagogy and Instruction Impact Engagement?

Chapter 3 outlined the evidence from this research that Chinese EMI lecturers in general tended to embrace expository in favour of constructivist teaching. Those in the humanities, social sciences and education academic disciplines were observed as aligning with a constructivist view reflected in problem-oriented instruction compared to those in the STEM disciplines who were consistently observed implementing topic-based instruction. In accordance with this finding, literature indicates (see

Chap. 1), that EMI lecturers are more likely to be predisposed to a 'one-way' transmission-orientation to their teaching, an approach which is argued by some researchers, as being largely the result of their low English proficiency (Huang, 2018; Lee, 2014; Yip & Tsang, 2007). However, this argument can be contradicted as there is no evidence indicating that EMI lecturers when using their first language (L1) show a clear-cut switch from expository to constructivist views and instruction. That is, lecturers who embrace topic- and teacher-directed approaches are not only those working in EMI contexts. Research supports this argument indicating that faculty lecturers teaching through English as their L1 do not necessarily fully embrace problem-oriented constructivist teaching, particularly at the undergraduate level (Smith et al., 2005). For example, a study conducted in the U.S.A reported that problem-oriented teaching is often introduced in the final year of undergraduate courses, and more notably in the STEM curriculum (Smith et al., 2005). It cannot be assumed that a constructivist pedagogy is being implemented on a large scale in all universities.

Literature is yet to confirm unequivocally that constructivist teaching is more effective than an expository method (Struyven et al., 2010) particularly with reference to student engagement. However, a number of empirical studies have flagged engagement as a key contributor to students' successful learning outcomes or achievements (Carini et al., 2006; Cross, 2005; Handelsman et al., 2005; Skinner et al., 1998; Smith et al., 2005; Zhao & Ku, 2004). The concept of engagement has also been theorized and debated as having a critical role in teaching and its multifaceted construct in nature (Kahu, 2013). The challenges in measuring engagement have also been an area of interest in past research (Furrer & Skinner, 2003; Mandernach, 2015). In EMI teaching it can be predicted that engagement becomes a particularly complex issue due to the inclusion of English as an additional language. As a more recent area of interest, there is a moderate amount of research (Huang, 2018; Lee, 2014; Yip & Tsang, 2007) reporting on the realities of engagement in EMI classes and lectures.

As a key component of instruction, engagement is addressed in both Merrill's (2002) First Principles of Instruction and Slavin's (1995) QAIT Instruction Model. Currently, there are a small number of studies having directly addressed EMI lecturers' engagement strategies. One study was conducted in a Korean university exploring the reasons why students were not active participants in class. It was found that EMI lecturers did not design learning activities and create interactive opportunities for students, and they were unable to produce meaningful questions when there were occasionally episodes of student engagement (Lee, 2014). Also, in Korea, Lim et al. (2021) conducted a survey of university students seeking opinions on the strategies and methods implemented by their lecturers that supported their engagement and motivation in online EMI classes. A key finding was that when EMI learners perceived care, warmth, encouragement and openness from their lecturers, they were more likely to participate in class. The shortfall in these data is that evidence on how the lecturers imparted these 'personality' traits which stimulated an engagement response from the students, is absent. In Europe, a study in Spain, reports a training program for EMI lecturers' professional development. This research invited the participating EMI lecturers to reflect on how to use semiotic resources to engage students through a proposed 'Pair/work engagement episodes framework'. Further exploration included how the EMI lecturers created engagement and paved the way towards competency in establishing multimodal interactional learning environments The research findings suggest that this competency will enable the lecturers to support students to move beyond passive learning towards being active classroom participants (Morell et al., 2022). There is potential for this recently developed framework to be implemented in actual EMI classrooms to provide an evidence base on its success or otherwise.

Based on the current literature, this Chapter explores and reports how engagement was enacted in the Chinese EMI lecturers' classes. Questions raised to guide the data collection were: Are there observable engagement designs in their lectures? If so, how are students specifically engaged? Are there any observable patterns in the lecturers' strategies for student engagement?

The following section delves into the conceptualization of 'engagement' to inform the data analysis.

## 4.2 Engagement as a Concept

Engagement is a complex concept having been defined by researchers from multiple perspectives. Some refer to engagement as "energy in action" and emphasize it as a "connection between person and activity" (Russell et al., 2005, p. 1), or "a person's active involvement during a task" (Reeve et al., 2004, p. 147). These definitions foreground 'active/activity' involving both physical and mental/psychological states. Others describe engagement as 'the time' learners spend undertaking a task and also their willingness to take part in activities (Mandernach, 2015; Stovall, 2003). This multifaceted notion of 'engagement' speaks to an agent's rational decisions around being task-ready and their dedication to follow through to completion. Still other researchers comprehend the concept from the perspective of outcomes achieved by the learners and the quality of the effort put into the learning activities to achieve these outcomes (Chen et al., 2008; Krause & Coates, 2008). To conceptualize the statements above, engagement is the amalgamation of physical and/or mental/cognitive activities situated in and supported by materials and/or people, through feeling, thinking and/or by doing. Engagement is therefore planned, purposeful activities where expected outcomes are a focus within the process.

For practical purposes, scholars have proposed that engagement is an umbrella term consisting of various sub-categories. Mandernach (2015, p. 5) has suggested, "…student engagement is a complex phenomenon that encompasses a range of behavioral, cognitive and affective components of the learning experience". Defining engagement as consisting of these three interrelated elements appears to be a widely held view in the literature (Fredricks, 2011; Fredricks et al., 2004).

The *emotional dimension* includes engaging positive feelings such as interest and curiosity about and reactions to academic content; happiness, and excitement when working with teachers and peers; and having a sense of belonging and connectedness to the class group and the institution (Fredricks, 2011; Fredricks et al., 2004). In a similar vein to the emotional/affective components of engagement, the term "psychological engagement" has been proposed when referring to "feelings of identification or belonging" towards one's school and class, and "relationships with teachers and peers" (Appleton et al., 2006, p. 429).

*Cognitive engagement* reflects the extent to which learners or participants think about and pay attention to, the learning activity, and how that translates to their attention and focus on the task at hand (Ben-Eliyahu et al., 2018). The processes at play in cognitive engagement have been described as containing internal indicators such as self-regulation and motivation and external indicators such as their academic achievement and performance, all of which reveal a learner's values, goals and autonomy towards a learning task (Appleton et al., 2006). Some researchers substantiate quality engagement occurs when students enact "higher-order thinking", "deep understanding of content and knowledge", "substantive discussion or conversation" and "metalanguage" (Munns et al., 2013, p. 28).

*Behavioral engagement* refers to people's physical involvement throughout and at the completion of an activity or task. This type of engagement can be more easily captured through observation. Fredricks et al. (2004) define it as: compliance to institutional and classroom norms such as following rules and policies; the absence of disruptive behaviors; and the presence of positive learning behaviors such as raising hands, asking questions and participating in class activities such as discussions; and attending extracurricular activities.

**Engagement in Learning**

The interconnectedness of each type of engagement and the subsequent impact on learning, is not without debate. Appleton et al. (2006, p. 431) emphasize the role of behavioral engagement and believe it is strongly connected to students' cognitive and psychological engagement. It needs to be noted that the 'activeness' identified in behavioral engagement does not automatically indicate or transpose to cognitive or emotional engagement. Emotional engagement does not guarantee active cognitive processing of content knowledge related to the learning task. Also, one could be active in thinking about the learning task and be experiencing emotions but may not be exhibiting behavioral engagement. Each type of engagement may operate independently of the other, or in any combination of the three at any one point in time.

Other researchers believe that emotional engagement is the key, and positive emotions lead to more positive behavioral and cognitive engagement, and an ensuing higher level of academic achievement (Frisby & Martin, 2010; Frisby & Myers, 2008; Glazier, 2016). Conversely "negative emotional information can overload and obstruct working memory, deteriorating attention to cognitive cues" (Douglas Fir Group, 2016, p. 35). It has also been expressed that a lack of emotional engagement can cause detachment from the ongoing activity, negatively impacting learning (Ben-Eliyahu & Linnenbrink-Garcia, 2013; Pekrun et al., 2009). However, there is also an opposing viewpoint that a propensity of emotional engagement can cause student complacency to the detriment of learning progress and could then be responsible for a compromized learning result (Carver & Scheier, 1990). Debates over the interconnection or disparity between behavioral, emotional and cognitive engagement reveal the concept's complicated nature.

The following section returns to the data collected in this research to investigate the Chinese lecturers' actual states of engagement in their EMI teaching.

## 4.3 Data – EMI Teaching and Engagement

Findings from the analysis of observation and field notes data, identified four categories of engagement strategies: cognitive, emotional, behavior (as proposed in much of the literature), and also managerial engagement. Cognitive engagement was most frequently used by the EMI lecturers, supplemented by the others. The STEM lecturers were observed engaging students logically with the content, through facilitating their cognitive thinking for the majority, if not all, of the available lecture time. EMI lecturers in the social sciences, humanities, and education utilized cognitive engagement strategies less frequently. However, across all disciplines, the time and effort dedicated to emotional, behavioral and managerial engagement was significantly less. Data from the stimulated recall interviews with EMI lecturers conducted immediately after the observations of their lectures has informed the explanation for this dominance of cognitive engagement strategies.

### 4.3.1 Cognitive Strategies – Chinese EMI Lecturers' Strength

Cognitive engagement activities were observed throughout the EMI lecturers' presentations, powerpoints and lecture time. As an overall observation this gave the impression that the EMI classes were rational, logical and inductive. Specific cognitive engagement strategies identified were memory association techniques, mind/concept mapping, deduction/induction, and providing cues and pauses to prompt and allow thinking time.

Memory association techniques provided sensory stimuli to connect students with the items or ideas that were being taught, for example when presenting new knowledge, some lecturers used diagrams and power point summaries to 'travel' back and stimulate the students' memory. Concept mapping was a strategy implemented frequently by these lecturers. During their presentations, the lecturers often wrote key ideas or concepts as the central term/word on a diagram and then radiating out from the center was the list of other related terms. This strategy consolidated cognitive learning by demonstrating how ideas and facts are related. There was an explicit intention on the part of the lecturers to map the connection between concepts visually, in order to help students better understand and recollect information. Deduction/induction through linguistic facilitation was another popular engagement strategy used by most of the lecturers (see also Chap. 6 Pragmatic Transfer).

Concept mapping and memory association strategies were often accompanied by cues and pauses when the lecturers noticed that some students looked puzzled or were without a response. In such situations, the lecturers were not prone to 'giving' the answers but offered prompts to engage the student's thinking towards a solution. These were observed as successful cognitive engagement strategies demonstrated by the lecturers during their presentations. To a lesser extent cognitive questioning and cognitive feedback were observed as engagement strategies by a few lecturers. Examples of the observed strategies are listed in Table 4.1 below.

Cognitive questioning and feedback were the two engagement strategies that were not used extensively or efficiently during the observed lectures. Cognitive questioning most notably occurred when the EMI lecturers intended to activate students' existing knowledge before delivering the new learning. Lower-order questioning such as 'what …where..' were posed in order to check students' immediate recall, however very few lecturers delivered higher-order questioning such as 'why' and 'how' questions, which position students with the responsibility to provide a comprehensive answer. Chin (2006) describes the notion of a 'cognitive ladder' to scaffold student understanding by progressing from lower-order to higher-order questioning. When engaging students with new content, lower-order questioning such as recall might be used; additionally, higher-order questioning could be followed when students' cognitive levels have increased or to guide them in that

**Table 4.1** Cognitive strategies demonstrated by EMI lecturers

| Cognitive activities | Examples observed | Frequency |
|---|---|---|
| Memory association techniques | During the lesson introduction, a mechanics professor asked students to recall the two concepts learned in the previous lecture. He used the association technique: Showing a picture of a crane and the Eiffel tower. Students started to murmur: Machinery and structure | Used by most of the lecturers |
| Mind mapping | A mechanics of materials lecturer listed types of material using a mind map, centering 'material' and then lines from the center indicating ceramic, metal, ore, polymer and enamel | Used by more than half the lecturers |
| Deduction/induction | A lecturer in computer sciences explained the concept 'algorithm' by giving examples, asking students to think about the commonalities and guiding them to conclude what an algorithm is. | Used by most of the lecturers |
| Cueing and pausing | The lecturer above from computer science allowed pauses and provided cues to aid in the understanding of the concept divide and conquer (think about when we have a very huge and complex problem to solve, what would be the first step.) | Used by most of the lecturers |
| Cognitive questioning | A chemistry lecturer asked students to check the 'other ingredients' and students called out: Acid, artificial color, antioxidant…. The lecturer asked: Can you think about and tell me whether these are essential and if yes, why? | Used by very few lecturers |
| Cognitive feedback | A lecturer from biology gave an elaboration and extension of a student's incomplete answer on stem cell after a general response to the student: 'ok'. | Used by very few lecturers |

direction. However, this was not the case in these observed lectures. Across either lower/higher-order questioning, lecturers provided very little scaffolding such as elaboration or rephrasing questions to facilitate students' comprehension during times when they were confused and/or failed to respond. The lack of scaffolding in the questioning strategies of these EMI lecturers could be explained from two perspectives: lecturers' capability to elaborate questions was being impacted by their English as the L2; as the majority of the Chinese lecturers implemented expository teaching, passing the responsibility for learning to students through advanced questioning was not a priority.

Cognitive feedback to students occurred very occasionally. In the observed lectures students were not provided with many opportunities to speak or perform. These EMI lecturers tended to provide general and brief feedback such as "alright" "ok" or "yeah". The observation data reveal that in-depth feedback that expanded the details of a student's answer was rare. Follow-up questioning and elaborate feedback can help stimulate and build students' various cognitive processes (Chin, 2006; Smart & Marshall, 2013). The interview data also indicate that the EMI lecturer's perceptions of their English L2 and the available lecture time impacted their use of cognitive engagement strategies, as demonstrated in the following excerpts.

> I don't have a lot of time and I need to cover the topics to introduce them to a complete course. Sometimes, you feel like asking students to work on things themselves but then you've lost time and can't finish as planned … Many things I could do but I choose not to because the class time is very limited (An Engineering Lecturer)

> EMI limits my freedom of teaching. I am much slower when explaining things in English. To put things together in the right words and right expressions is a burden. Sometimes I feel a terrible expression is worse than no explanation. (A Medical Science Lecturer)

## 4.3.2 Emotional Engagement – Distancing Students for Complex Reasons

Throughout the observations of the EMI lecturers' teaching, field notes focussing on the learning environments were recorded. Most of the EMI lecturers established learning environments that were more rational than emotional, more intense than relaxed, and more uninspired than exciting. Greetings can be a starting point to engage students emotionally. Data reveal that very few lecturers welcomed students with greetings such as "how are you?" to relax the atmosphere or to exhibit a sense of caring for students. Lectures typically commenced with, "ok, today, I am going to introduce you to …". The tone was calm and flat, and no excitement or emotional connection or rapport was observed as a concerted effort being made on the part of the lecturers. However, there were a few lecturers who utilized more inclusive expressions such as 'Today, we are going to learn…'. Whether consciously or subconsciously, the use of "I" in the main position for the action "teach" or "introduce", delegates passivity to the students as they are in the secondary position in relation to the action. Psychologically, the use of 'I' denotes a division between the lecturers and their students. In this way teachers are positioning themselves as the knowledge holders, further signifying their commitment to expository teaching and topic-based knowledge dissemination. This finding confers with Han and Han's (2019) research that Chinese teachers were predisposed to establishing an hierarchical relationship with students.

The establishment or distancing of lecturer and student via the language expressed has been discussed in Chap. 3 as indicative of tenor in communication. Tenor is identifiable and, in this research, almost all the lecturers distanced themselves from their students by using formal, impersonal language and at the onset, established themselves as the expert. In addition to the tenor in the communication itself other strategies also contribute to student/lecturer relationships. Initiating positive feedback also has a key role. Cognitive feedback, or the lack thereof in this research, was discussed in the section 'Cognitive Engagement' above in terms of its potential to improve learning and raised again here to consider the opportunity afforded feedback to establish rapport and a positive connection with students. The feedback delivered by the EMI lecturers was observed to be perfunctory when responding to students who were performing well and at the same time, little sympathy was shown to those students offering incorrect answers or struggling with understanding. The responses were brief and general with no further details or praise for students. Feedback such as "correct", "good" or "yes" were common. For underperforming students, most of the lecturers either said "No!" or simply ignored that student and turned to another. Little emotional support or encouragement were observed. Rewarding the 'right' and punishing the 'wrong' in response to students' performance is the type of feedback promoted decades ago in the West (Langer, 2011). This model continues into current practice for Chinese teachers. In Han and Yao's (2013) study, a divergence in feedback identified was that Western (Australian local) teachers tended to provide genuine feedback, focussing on the issue or the answer, and acknowledged effort; comparatively Chinese background teachers tended to show no compassion to students' poor performance. This issue was discussed with the participating EMI lecturers in this research at the conclusion of the observed lectures and a sample of their opinions are recorded below:

> ... Being nice to them is not always helpful for their learning. Once you start to be lenient, it's the time they are getting relaxed and less pressured. But life is tough and I have to train them to be tough. (A Mechanic Engineering lecturer)

> When they answered the question wrong, that means they didn't review their lesson properly, and why would you want to make them comfortable? (An International Relationship Lecturer)

> I have too much to cover throughout this subject and I am only given certain hours to complete it. On many occasions, I have to be in a rush and cannot dwell on things other than the content. They are adults and they understand this. (A Physics Lecturer)

The excerpts provided by these lecturers exposed a predisposition towards 'tough love' in their teaching. Some lecturers reinforced their power in the learning environment through less sympathetic and less encouraging language however their intention was to influence the students towards self-disciplined learning with successful outcomes, even if this meant 'stressing' the students. Whilst, literature reports positive emotional engagement and establishing rapport with students can relax students and provide an environment conducive to learning, these Chinese lecturers, believed negative or no emotional interaction can motivate students to apply themselves and achieve the desired outcomes. Anecdotally this view appears to be widely shared amongst Chinese teacher communities. For other lecturers, the crowded curriculum accounts for the fact that interaction and engagement is viewed as extraneous to the key business of teaching – desirable but extravagant in practice.

#### 4.3.2.1 Rare Engagement Through Humor and Personal Narratives

Research across various fields of study signals the use of humor and sharing of personal stories as useful strategies for emotional engagement (Heyward, 2010; Hoad et al., 2013). These can reduce tension in classrooms and positively improve students' cognitive learning. In this research the use of humor was not observed and there was a permeating strict and stern phenomenon operating in most of the observed classes. This research appears to parallel notions such as "humor has been traditionally given little respect in Chinese culture mainly due to the Confucian emphasis on keeping proper manners in social interactions" (Yue, 2010, p. 403, cited in Wu & Chan, 2013, p. 1050).

Similarly, sharing personal narratives was not a common strategy, however one example was noted. A Computer Science lecturer included a personal account as an engagement strategy with her second-year students. At the commencement of her lecture a typical Western style greeting was offered. She then requested the students' permission to sit down for the lecture as she had a painful ankle. Students expressed understanding with many suggesting she should sit immediately. Sharing her personal experience with students established her as sincere and approachable contributing to an harmonious atmosphere. It was also noticeable that she had already established a positive rapport with the group. In the stimulated recall interview after her teaching, she explained that she received three degrees in Canada including her PhD degree which may help explain her successful strategies to engage students. This strategy was a rarity in the lectures observed.

#### 4.3.2.2 Emotional Engagement Through Moral Education

A more prevalent strategy of emotional engagement was when the EMI lecturers used 'moral education' to make connections with students. An example being one lecturer who raised "*jia guo qing huai*" (translation: the love and affection attached to one's nation and country), appealing to students' nationalistic pride. He encouraged students to study hard, to compete with peers in the U.S.A., to secure President Xi Jinping's pride. The students were noted to respond with interest, watching and listening carefully. Western teacher-student or lecturer-students' emotional engagement is situated in a context of a more equitable relationship, whereas the Chinese

EMI lecturer-students' emotional engagement, to some extent, had overtones of a relationship akin to that of a parent, role model and authority figure. There is literature reporting this phenomenon throughout the different sectors of Chinese education (Han, 2020; Li & Du, 2013).

### 4.3.3  Limited Behavioral and Managerial Engagement

In terms of the physical dynamics within the lecture rooms, in this study, the majority were static and passive with minimal movement. The lecturers not only distanced the students in terms of the tenor of the communication, but this was reinforced by an accompanying physical distance. Lecturers were not observed freely moving in and around the room. Instead, they mostly stood next to the lectern, where the IT was set up and close to the PPT screen. Some consistently referred to and read notes associated with the PPT slides whereas the instruction of others was to read from the PPT slides, totally, for the duration of the lecture. This lecturing style was also accompanied by moments when they focused their gaze away from the screen to a point in the room or into the air. No eye contact with students was observed. From their oral English it was deduced that English as the medium caused a cognitive overload – that language translation was at the forefront of their thoughts reflected in their actions. This deduction was supported by the observation of those who also provided the same lecture in Chinese to a different student cohort. During these lectures there was noticeably more physical movement and behavioral engagement on the part of the lecturers.

The data also reveal a modest use of managerial engagement, such as the lecturers organizing the students through instructions such as "Now you can have a discussion with the person next to you." It was noticeable that the students did not always respond to the lecturers' questions as illustrated in the data excerpts below. In the stimulated recall interviews, conducted after the observed lectures, some lecturers expressed their frustration at the students' silences to questioning, as they could not gauge the students understanding or progress through the lecture. For example:

T: "Did you read the two articles I sent you?"
S: …. (Silence).
T: "Did you? Did you?"
S: …. (No answer). (International Relationship lecture)
T: "Do you follow me?"
S: …. (No answer)
T. "Do you follow me?"
S: …. (No answer)
T: "So you cannot follow me?... Just speak out if you can't. It doesn't matter."
S: …. (No answer). (Physics lecture)

This research found that within the four types of engagement, the most commonly implemented was cognitive engagement. The lecturers demonstrated multiple strategies to engage students cognitively to scaffold their understanding of content learning. However, strategies for emotional, behavioral and managerial/administrative engagement were underdeveloped and/or believed less important in contributing to learning.

## 4.4 Linguistic Features in Engagement Activities

Some linguistic features were identified within the EMI lecturers' engagement language. Firstly, some lecturers showed 'weak instructional signs'. In these instances, there was a tendency to use auxiliary verbs and thinking verbs when requesting or expecting an action. For example, "you can…" and "I think…" were common as sentence starters (Table 4.2: Column A). These expressions could have confused students as the use of auxiliary verbs alluded to a choice in willingness and softened the obligations on students to commence the actions or activities. In contrast there were lecturers, albeit a few, who were aware of the need to start a request with an action verb, for example, "now turn to …" and "now explain…" (Table 4.2: Column B). Instructional signs need to be very clear, specific action verbs in EMI lectures to circumvent students not responding as intended by the lecturers.

Secondly, the use of personal pronouns in the lecturers' expressions tended to establish a division between lecturer and student as mentioned earlier. In attempting to verify students' understanding , some allocated the students to the subject position. Examples were "Are you clear?" or "Do you understand?"; others framed themselves as the subject, evident in the expressions, "Have I confused you?" or "Am I clear?". Both signify who is responsible for the problem solving. The excerpts in Table 4.3: Column A indicate the students are the owner of problems implying they are responsible for their problems or confusion. The examples quoted in Table 4.3: Column B indicates that the lecturers have created the problem and need to take responsibility to provide further clarification. This differential use of pronouns in the instructional language signifies the type of relationship the EMI lecturers prefer to establish with their students. It reflects their pedagogical view which directed them to use teacher-centered or learner-centered instruction.

**Table 4.2** Instructional signs

| A | B |
|---|---|
| You *can* share your ideas with your classmates now | Now *turn to* the person next to you and *explain to* the person your understanding of… |
| I *think* you can discuss with your peers now about this question | Now *explain* your understanding to someone next to you for 3 min |

**Table 4.3** Divisiveness in the use of pronouns

| A | B |
|---|---|
| Do you understand? | Have I confused you? |
| Are you clear? | Am I clear? |

Thirdly, the overuse of an interpersonal pronoun by some lecturers was noted when experiential themes were addressed. Specifically, when some lecturers explained subject knowledge, or an issue, matter or concept, there was a tendency to add a personal pronoun as the starting point and subject of the sentence. For example, starting the sentence with "We, You, I", rather than having a verb to start a request for action, resulted in expressions such as, "I would like you to…". Another example of the overuse of pronouns was one lecturer's statement: "If we add fine chemicals in our food, our food will not go bad quickly" when it could have been more simply put, 'fine chemicals can preserve the food'. The inclusion of additional interpersonal vocabulary can extend and complicate the communication and may disrupt students from comprehending the targeted content. In the stimulated recall interviews, some lecturers expressed that they were not aware of the use of personal pronouns as a means to engage students and had been concerned to include them in order to construct grammatically correct sentences following the subject-verb structure.

## 4.5 Discussion – Engagement, Language and Tenor?

Scholars of engagement studies have also elaborated the importance of quality engagement across all categories and within all learning contexts (Ben-Eliyahu et al., 2018; Munns et al., 2013). Other research has particularly promoted the role of emotional engagement in cognition (Ben-Eliyahu & Linnenbrink-Garcia, 2013; Douglas Fir Group, 2016; Okon-Singer et al., 2015). Studies focusing on emotional engagement indicate that emotional cues, emotional states, and emotional traits may strongly influence information processing, attention, working memory, and cognitive control (Okon-Singer et al., 2015). Under the concept of rapport, emotional connection and well-established rapport is endorsed as a strategy to reduce anxiety, encourage interaction and increase student participation (Frisby & Martin, 2010). It is believed to have "a strong, significant, and consistently positive effect in helping students to learn" (Glazier, 2016, p. 438). It is also argued that students who are emotionally connected well with the teacher, tend to concentrate better in class and more often have a down-to-earth attitude to learning (Frisby & Martin, 2010; Frisby & Myers, 2008).

Such research findings contend high quality emotional engagement assists students to think capably and creatively, feel contentment when at school and be motivated to achieve the desired learning goals. This engagement literature can be seen to generate two assumptions: quality engagement necessarily requires lecturers or teachers to engage students with each type of engagement (cognition, emotion, and behavioral, and/or management); the importance of emotional engagement cannot be understated and is needed for genuine learning to take place. In addition, a third assumption is specific to EMI research which claims that quality engagement is lacking in EMI programs due to the EMI lecturers' English proficiency (Huang, 2018; Yip & Tsang, 2007).

The findings from this research do not reinforce these assumptions. Through analyzing the observations of actual teaching/lecturing episodes and the interview data, it was found that all of the lecturers utilized cognitive engagement substantially, whereas very few enacted emotional, behavioral and managerial engagement. Their lectures followed a rational format and squarely focused on the objectives to instil the discipline knowledge and content in the most efficient manner possible. As this was observably teacher-directed through the various strategies of cognitive engagement enacted, it further strengthens the finding that most EMI lecturers embraced expository teaching. In contrast they did not demonstrate rich strategies of emotional engagement. The EMI learning environment for the students could be described as dull and at times stressful. There was no excitement around the teaching and learning observed on the part of either the lecturers or the students. However, this is not to argue that a lack of emotional engagement necessarily equates to low learning performance. This study did not aim to assess, if or how, emotional engagement impacts on cognitive learning in terms of students' achieving their current unit learning outcomes and seeking the student perspective was beyond the scope of this research. Interview data captured the perspectives of EMI lecturers that Chinese students should be trained to be 'tough' and stress resistant, and able to concentrate on cognitive learning in the absence of emotional engagement.

This perspective does seem to impact negatively on the world stage as even though Chinese classes are reported as demonstrating limited teacher-student rapport and emotional engagement, as with the findings in this study, students' learning outcomes are as competitive or leading, in measures of academic outcomes around the globe. This echoes some researchers' arguments: it is common that Chinese students can develop a high tolerance for stress, anxiety, and other negative emotions (Lu et al., 2015), and negative emotions such as stress can have positive impact on some mature aged students' learning outcomes (Bisson, 2017). In the context of mature learners, it is arguably the case that successful learning does not necessarily rely on emotional engagement.

## 4.6 Conclusion

This Chapter analyzed the engagement features demonstrated by the participating EMI lecturers during their subject teaching. The conclusion drawn from the data is that Chinese EMI lecturers did not develop and give equal priority to each type of engagement. On the contrary, they were all observed to focus on cognitive engagement with very little evidence of emotional, behavior and managerial engagement. It is proposed that this finding is an outcome of the discipline area in which they taught as well as a reflection of the teaching ideology of the lecturers, the majority of whom are committed to an expository pedagogical perspective. English as the language of instruction contributed in a lesser way to the lack of concern for behavioral, emotional and managerial engagement.

# References

Appleton, J., Christenson, S., Kim, D., & Reschly, A. (2006). Measuring cognitive and psychological engagement: Validation of the student engagement instrument. *Journal of School Psychology, 44*, 427–445.
Ben-Eliyahu, A., & Linnenbrink-Garcia, L. (2013). Extending self-regulated learning to include self-regulated emotion strategies. *Motivation and Emotion, 37*, 558–573. https://doi.org/10.1007/s11031-012-9332-3
Ben-Eliyahu, A., Moore, D., Dorph, R., & Schunn, C. (2018). Investigating the multidimensionality of engagement: Affective, behavioral, and cognitive engagement across science activities and contexts. *Contemporary Educational Psychology, 53*, 87–105.
Bisson, K. H. (2017). *The effect of anxiety and depression on college students' academic performance: Exploring social support as a moderator.* Electronic Thesis: Abilene Christian University: Digital Commons @ ACU. https://digitalcommons.acu.edu/cgi/viewcontent.cgi?article=1057&context=etd
Carini, R. M., Kuh, G. D., & Klein, S. P. (2006). Student engagement and student learning: Testing the linkages. *Research in Higher Education, 47*(1), 1–32.
Carver, C., & Scheier, M. (1990). Origins and functions of positive and negative affect: A control-process view. *Psychological Review, 97*(1), 19–35. https://doi.org/10.1037/0033-295X.97.1.19
Chen, P.-S., Gonyea, R., & Kuh, G. (2008). Learning at a distance. *Journal of Online Education, 4*(3). http://innovateonline.info/index.php?view=article&id=438&action=login.
Chin, C. (2006). Classroom interaction in science: Teacher questioning and feedback to students' responses. *International Journal of Science Education, 28*(11), 1315–1346. https://doi.org/10.1080/09500690600621100
Cross, K. P. (2005). *What do we know about students' learning and how do we know it?* Center for the Study of Higher Education Research and Occasional Paper Series. Retrieved from http://www.aahe.org/nche/cross_lecture.htm
Douglas Fir Group. (2016). A transdisciplinary framework for SLA in a multilingual world. *The Modern Language Journal, 100*(Supplement, 2016), 19–47.
Fredricks, J. A. (2011). Engagement in school and out of school contexts: A multidimensional view of engagement. *Theory into Practice, 4*, 327–335.
Fredricks, J., Blumenfeld, P., & Paris, A. (2004). School engagement: Potential of the concept, state of the evidence. *Review of Educational Research, 74*(1), 59–109.
Frisby, B., & Martin, M. (2010). Instructor–student and student–student rapport in the classroom. *Communication Education, 59*(2), 146–164. https://doi.org/10.1080/03634520903564362
Frisby, B., & Myers, S. (2008). The relationships among perceived instructor rapport, student participation, and student learning outcomes. *Texas Speech Communication Journal, 33*(1), 27–34.
Furrer, C., & Skinner, E. (2003). Sense of relatedness as a factor in children's academic engagement and performance. *Journal of Educational Psychology, 95*, 148–162.
Glazier, R. (2016). Building rapport to improve retention and success in online classes. *Journal of Political Science Education, 12*(4), 437–456. https://doi.org/10.1080/15512169.2016.1155994
Han, J. (2020), *Theorising culture: A Chinese perspective*. Palgrave Pivot. DOI: https://doi.org/10.1007/978-3-030-23880-3.

# References

Han, J., & Han, Y. (2019). Cultural concepts as powerful theoretical tools: Chinese teachers' perceptions of their relationship with students in a cross-cultural context. *International Journal for the Scholarship of Teaching and Learning, 13*(1), 1–9. https://doi.org/10.20429/ijsotl.2019.130108

Han, J., & Yao, J. (2013). A case study of bilingual student-teachers' classroom English: Applying the education-linguistic model. *Australian Journal of Teacher Education, 38*(2), 118–131.

Handelsman, M., Briggs, W., Sullivan, N., & Towler, A. (2005). A measure of college student course engagement. *The Journal of Educational Research, 98*(3), 184–192. https://doi.org/10.3200/JOER.98.3.184-192

Heyward, P. (2010). Emotional engagement through Drama: Strategies to assist learning through role-play. *International Journal of Teaching and Learning in Higher Education, 22*(2), 197–204.

Hoad, C., Deed, C., & Lugg, A. (2013). The potential of humor as a trigger for emotional engagement in outdoor education. *The Journal of Experimental Education*. https://doi.org/10.1177/1053825913481583

Huang, Y. (2018). Learner resistance to English-medium instruction practices: A qualitative case study. *Teaching in Higher Education, 23*(4), 435–449. https://doi.org/10.1080/13562517.2017.1421629

Kahu, E. (2013). Framing student engagement in higher education. *Studies in Higher Education, 38*(5), 758–773. https://doi.org/10.1080/03075079.2011.598505

Krause, K.-L., & Coates, H. (2008). Students' engagement in first-year university. *Assessment & Evaluation in Higher Education, 33*(5), 493–505. https://doi.org/10.1080/02602930701698892

Langer, P. (2011). The use of feedback in education: A complex instructional strategy. *Psychological Reports, 109*(3), 775–784.

Lee, G. (2014). Why students don't participate in English medium instruction classes in a Korean university: A case study. *English Teaching, 69*(1), 91–117.

Li, H., & Du, X.-Y. (2013). Confronting cultural challenges when reconstructing the teacher-student relationship in a Chinese context. In J. Kirkebaek, X. Du, & A. Jensen (Eds.), *Teaching and learning: Negotiating the context* (pp. 79–94). Brill.

Lim, H., Murdoch, Y., & Cho, J. (2021). Online EMI learner engagement and perceptions of teaching and learning during the COVID-19 pandemic. *Innovations in Education and Teaching International*. https://doi.org/10.1080/14703297.2021.1905030

Lu, W., Bian, Q., Song, Y., Ren, J., Xu, X., & Zhao, M. (2015). Prevalence and related risk factors of anxiety and depression among Chinese college freshmen. *Journal of Huazhong University of Science and Technology [Medical Sciences], 35*(6), 815–822. https://doi.org/10.1007/s11596-015-1512-4

Mandernach, J. (2015). Assessment of student engagement in higher education: A synthesis of literature and assessment tools. *International Journal of Learning, Teaching and Educational Research, 12*(2), 1–14.

Merrill, D. (2002). First principles of instruction. *Educational Technology Research and Development, 50*(3), 43–59. https://doi.org/10.1007/BF02505024

Morell, T., Beltrán-Palanques, V., & Norte, N. (2022). Multimodal analysis of pair work engagement episodes: Implications for EMI lecturer training. *Journal of English for Academic Purposes, 58*(101124).

Munns, G., Sawyer, W., & Cole, B. (2013). *Exemplary teachers of students in poverty*. Taylor and Francis Group.

Okon-Singer, H., Hendler, T., Pessoa, L., & Shackman, A. (2015). The neurobiology of emotion–cognition interactions: Fundamental questions and strategies for future research. *Frontiers in Human Neuroscience, 9*(Article 58), 1–14.

Pekrun, R., Elliot, A., & Maier, M. (2009). Achievement goals and achievement emotions: Testing a model of their joint relations with academic performance. *Journal of Educational Psychology, 101*(1), 115–135. https://doi.org/10.1037/a0013383

Reeve, J., Jang, H., Carrell, D., Jeon, S., & Barch, J. (2004). Enhancing students' engagement by increasing teachers' autonomy support. *Motivation and Emotion, 28*, 147–169.

Russell, J., Ainley, M., & Frydenberg, E. (2005). *Schooling issues digest: Student motivation and engagement*. Australian Government, Department of Education Science and Training.

Skinner, E. A., Zimmer-Gembeck, M. J., Connell, J., Eccles, J., & Wellborn, J. (1998). Individual differences and the development of perceived control. *Monographs of the Society for Research in Child Development, 63*(2–3). https://doi.org/10.2307/1166220

Slavin, R. (1995). A model of effective instruction. *The Educational Forum, 59*(2), 166–176. https://doi.org/10.1080/00131729509336383

Smart, J., & Marshall, J. (2013). Interactions between classroom discourse, teacher questioning, and student cognitive engagement in middle school science. *Journal of Science Teacher Education, 24*(2), 249–267. https://doi.org/10.1007/s10972-012-9297-9

Smith, K., Sheppard, S., Johnson, D., & Johnson, R. (2005). Pedagogies of engagement: Classroom-based practices. *Journal of Engineering Education, 87–101*. https://doi.org/10.1002/j.2168-9830.2005.tb00831.x

Stovall, I. (2003). Engagement and online learning. *UIS Community of Practice for E-Learning*. http://otel.uis.edu/copel/EngagementandOnlineLearning.ppt,

Struyven, K., Dochy, F., & Janssens, S. (2010). Teach as you preach: The effects of student-Centred versus lecture-based teaching on student teachers' approaches to teaching. *European Journal of Teacher Education, 33*(1), 43–64.

Wu, J., & Chan, R. (2013). Chines teachers' use of humour in coping with stress. *International Journal of Psychology, 48*(6), 1050–1056.

Yip, D., & Tsang, W. (2007). Evaluation of the effects of the medium of instruction on science learning of Hong Kong secondary students: Students' self-concept in science. *International Journal of Science and Mathematics Education, 5*, 393–413. https://doi.org/10.1007/s10763-006-9043-x

Yue, X. D. (2010). Exploration of Chinese humor: Historical review, empirical findings, and critical reflections. *Humor, 23*, 403–420.

Zhao, C., & Kuh, G. (2004). Adding value: Learning communities and student engagement. *Research in Higher Education, 45*, 115–138.

**Open Access** This chapter is licensed under the terms of the Creative Commons Attribution 4.0 International License (http://creativecommons.org/licenses/by/4.0/), which permits use, sharing, adaptation, distribution and reproduction in any medium or format, as long as you give appropriate credit to the original author(s) and the source, provide a link to the Creative Commons license and indicate if changes were made.

The images or other third party material in this chapter are included in the chapter's Creative Commons license, unless indicated otherwise in a credit line to the material. If material is not included in the chapter's Creative Commons license and your intended use is not permitted by statutory regulation or exceeds the permitted use, you will need to obtain permission directly from the copyright holder.

# Chapter 5
# Cross-Linguistic Influence: Bilingual EMI Lecturers' English and Chinese Entwined

**Abstract** In the previous two Chapters, the pedagogical ideology of the participating lecturers and the subsequent reality of their 'instruction' and 'engagement' was examined. From a psycholinguistic perception this Chapter focuses on the Chinese lecturers' L1-influenced English in their teaching. The data indicates that cross-linguistic influence was the cognitive reality for the EMI lecturers and provided a scaffolding role in their teaching. This research suggests that although the EMI lecturers' L1 and L2 are two genetically distant languages, they were interdependent and formed a stable construct that served as a powerful language resource in their teaching. Theoretically, this Chapter moves beyond a structuralist view of judging language transfer as right or wrong, correct or incorrect, perfect or deficit. It has implemented a post-structuralist interpretation of this phenomenon by proposing 'explicit' and 'implicit' transfer and acknowledging L1-influenced EMI lecturers' English as a temporary form of languaging within the translaguaging process.

**Keywords** Cross-linguistic influence · L1/L2 transfer · Translanguaging · Explicit transfer · Implicit transfer

## 5.1 Introduction

As discussed in Chap. 1, the English use of EMI lecturers and students has attracted much attention in studies of English as a Medium of Instruction (Ball & Linday, 2013; Council of Europe, 2001; Danish Language Council, 2012; Jiang et al., 2019; Klaassen & Räsänen, 2006). This issue has created tension for institutions offering EMI programs (Costa & Coleman, 2013; Dearden, 2014, 2015, 2016; Werther et al., 2014), in that stipulating English capability is an important criterion when recruiting EMI lecturers (Dearden, 2014). Couched within a monolingual framework such research has proposed much EMI teaching to be void of authentic colloquial English, compounded by grammatical problems in oral presentations and lectures, and framed the issue as an English language deficiency on the part of EMI lecturers. This is understandable as tension may arise for all stakeholders when an academic subject is taught through a lecturer's additional language.

In parallel with the research on monolingual priorities, literature has also reported the influence of lecturers' and students' L1 on EMI teaching and learning but from the contrasting position of translanguaging (Lin & Lo, 2017; Macaro et al., 2020; Pun & Macaro, 2019; Sah & Li, 2022; Tai & Li, 2021). For example, Lin and Lo (2017) studied school teachers' CLIL classes in Hong Kong, with the conclusion that when students drew on their daily life experiences, connecting their everyday L1 language they were more effectively able to engage in co-constructing knowledge in an EMI class. In Mainland China, Macaro et al. (2020) studied Chinese and English use in Chinese EMI classes. This research reported that in the observed classes the participating lecturers used 'English-only' for 99% of the teaching time. The findings also outlined that students preferred English instruction throughout the lectures, with L1 use preferred only for scaffolding their understanding. These findings imply that either the EMI lecturers and/or the institutions, hold a monolingual view in terms of EMI programs. It may also indicate that EMI, is understood as 'teaching in English only' based on the widely accepted translation of the term (*quan ying shou ke* – teaching 'teaching totally in English') (see Chap. 2). Further Pun and Macaro (2019) studied L1 and English use in EMI classes in school contexts in Hong Kong. This research identified that a shift between L1 and English impacted on the quality of classroom interactions: when lecturers used L2 English, the students became less interactive; and when L1 was used during instruction, the teachers were able to ask more challenging questions to promote higher-order thinking.

This research is noteworthy given the majority, if not all, EMI lecturers and perhaps students, are bilingual or multilingual, and therefore their English is not insulated from their L1. The focus of this Chapter is psycholinguistic in nature and from a cognitive perspective it offers insights into how the L1 of these Chinese EMI lecturers influenced their teaching and instructional language in English. In practice bi/multilinguals cognitively, and arguably naturally, activate their repertoire of background language/s when using English (Gunnarsson et al., 2015). Although English is the 'official' instructional language, EMI lecturers' bi/multilingual reality implies that cross-linguistic transfer is an inevitable phenomenon in EMI classrooms. This Chapter is concerned with the interrelationship between the lecturers' two languages, and the mechanisms for how L1 cognitively assists with the scaffolding of the EMI lecturers' construction and use of their L2. Data in this research reveal the L1's phonetic, semantic, syntactic, conceptual and, to a lesser extent, pragmatic influence during EMI teaching.[1]

Cross-linguistic influence is a meaningful lens through which to explore the teaching of the EMI lecturers participating in this research. It is not the intention of this Chapter to examine the EMI lecturers' L1/L2 language transfer as positive or negative or to judge their English as deficient or incorrect as advocates of structuralism would propose. Rather, this Chapter has sought to identify the various types of

---

[1] It should be noted that pragmatic influence is often related to how the broader contexts, such as social and cultural, of an L1 influences L2 production. This is reported in a subsequent chapter (see Chap. 6).

transfer and the linguistic features generated by observing the actual EMI teaching of the research participants. It aims to identify how the various categories of transfer has functioned as a steppingstone or a self-scaffolding strategy for their instructional language development.

## 5.2 Cross-Linguistic Influence

Cross-linguistic influence (CLI) is a language phenomenon bilinguals or multilinguals experience during the cognitive processes occurring in language use (Cenoz, 2003; Cook, 2003; Jarvis, 2016; Odlin, 2005; Pavenko, 2000; Pavlenko & Jarvis, 2002). Linguists traditionally organize transfer into categories such as "phonemic, morphological, lexical, semantic, conceptual, syntactic, discursive, pragmatic, and collocational" (Jarvis & Pavlenko, 2008, p. 2). To categorize further, language transfer may occur at linguistic levels such as language forms (for example, the phonological, morphological or syntactic structure) and then also at the level of the meanings associated with those forms (for example, lexical, semantic or conceptual). It may also occur at a non-linguistic level, that is, transfer of pragmatic functions (discursive, pragmatic or collocational). Cummins (2008) highlights non-linguistic transfer such as pragmatic transfer (for example, the use of paralinguistic features such as gestures to aid communication) and transfer of metacognitive and metalinguistic strategies (for example, strategies of visualising, the use of graphic organizers, mnemonic devices, and vocabulary acquisition strategies). For the Chinese EMI lecturers in this research, their language transfer could hence be considered as involving the application of linguistic or non-linguistic rules from L1 to their English use, or in reverse, L2 back to their L1.

### 5.2.1 Negative vs Positive or Explicit vs Implicit Transfer

In the dominant discourse surrounding L1 and L2 transfer, a negativity towards this phenomenon exists. Literature has more commonly reported negative transfer as it appears overtly, in the form of errors, whereas positive transfer is implicit, mostly unnoticed in practice, and therefore less discussed and reported in the literature (Jarvis, 2016; Jarvis & Pavlenk, 2008; Lennon, 2008). Whilst this negative view narrowly focuses on communication errors, at the same time it enacts a silence around the positive function transfer can bring from across bilinguals' language experiences. Ringbom (2006, p. 31) critiqued the truism that "if a learner produces an unacceptable word or construction of any kind, some degree of ignorance lies behind it". To mitigate the negativity of transfer, from the learners' perspectives, he proposed transfer should utilize the "perceived and assumed" cross-linguistic similarities. Ringbom (2006) argues that transfer tends to be positive when it is clearly manifested in comprehension across languages, especially for those perceived to be similar; it is negative when L1 and L2 differences create interference in the learner's L2. Thus, "it is natural to perceive similarities across closely-related languages, and they are especially frequently employed in comprehension" (Ringbom, 2006, p. 26).

Applying this 'relational languages' proposition, Chinese and English would be categorized as distant languages. On many occasions, similarities may be less obvious but more assumed by the Chinese English bilinguals. It would be less likely that positive transfer will occur between English and Chinese and it would be commonplace for errors in English L2 production due to the influence of Chinese as the L1. This structuralist perspective is problematic. It foregrounds the language form, and negates the functions transfer offers to bilinguals in their cognitive abilities across both languages. Proponents of 'negative' transfer are basically focussing on the explicit or observable language examples, whereas 'positive' acknowledges one language can be merged into another for a range of purposes, implicitly or covertly. The use of the terms 'explicit' and 'implicit' transfer is offered in this research as this gives voice to the agency of the EMI lecturers, and acknowledges the facilitative role of L1/L2 transfer in the teaching and learning process.

By describing transfer as 'explicit' or 'implicit' rather than negative or positive, theoretically, this confronts the structuralist view that there is a 'black and white' positing within the world and negates judgement of language transfer as right or wrong, correct or incorrect, perfect or deficit. It enlists a post-structuralist perspective, and in this context accepts that there can be a variety of English or Englishes. Categorizing transfer as 'explicit' or 'implicit' is to give L1-influenced Chinese EMI lecturers' English a legitimate status. Thus, 'explicit' or 'implicit' transfer is one type of translanguaging and one sub-concept under the translanguaging umbrella. It is a temporary form and outcome of languaging in the translaguaging process.[2]

## 5.3 L1-Influenced English Identified in the EMI Lecturers' Teaching

This section draws on observational evidence to examine the influence of the L1 Chinese language on the EMI lecturers' use of English. The data reveal that explicit transfer between the EMI lecturers' L1 to L2 was substantially mobilized. Reliance on L2 may have illustrated the demographics of this particular group of EMI lecturers, that is, being experts in a discipline other than English (ESL) and without extensive English as L2 education in or throughout their career. This echoes the finding of a recent research study that claims the propensity to explicit transfer between EMI lecturers' L1 and L2 is related to the degree of formal, intensive language skills

---

[2] Transfer is a psycholinguistic concept. It has the capacity to address the relationship between EMI lecturers' cognition and their two languages; translanguaging is a sociolinguistic concept. It is used to address the relationship between the EMI lecturers' two languages and their learners. EMI lecturers' translanguaging practice is explored in Chap. 7.

## 5.3 L1-Influenced English Identified in the EMI Lecturers' Teaching

training provided to them (Babaii & Ramazani, 2017). In the case of this research (L1 Chinese/L2 English), the language transfer exhibited by the EMI lecturers did not follow a single linear mode but was rather indicative of a multifaceted process. Different patterns of interdependence were observed across L1 and L2. Among the various types of explicit transfer, the most common types were phonological, syntactic and semantic transfers. Whilst there was evidence of conceptual and reverse transfer, these incidences were substantially less frequent. It needs to be noted also, that non-linguistic (pragmatic or metalinguistic) transfer was also operationalized. This phenomenon is analyzed in Chap. 6.

### 5.3.1 Phonological Influence – Consonants, Vowels and Consonant-Vowel Complex

Data demonstrate frequent use of phonological transfer in the EMI lecturers' instructional English. This was an observed trend for all the lecturers including those more fluent in English usage. English consonants and vowels that are absent in Chinese (the L1 for these research participants), and those words that end with friction consonants were noted as the majority of explicit transfer cases. Examples from the observational data appear in Table 5.1.

Attributable to the absence of these English consonants such as interdental fricative /ð/ and /θ/, palatal affricate /dʒ/, /tʃ/ and tr/, and alveolar lateral /l/ in the Chinese pronunciation system, the EMI lecturers notably replaced these with comparable Chinese interdental fricatives [z] and [s], palatal glide [j], palatal affricates [ch] and [q] and palatal rhotic [r] (Table 5.1: Columns 1 and 2). The English vowels /u/, /eɪ/, /e/, /ʌ/, /æ/, /eə/, /aɪ/ were substituted with Chinese[u:], [yi], [ə], [a], [ai], [ai], [a] in some lecturers' pronunciations (Table 5.1: Columns 3 and 4). It was also observed that a significant proportion of the lecturers tended to add the vowel sounds [ə] and/or [i:] to those English words ending with fricative consonants such as /f/, /t/, /d/and /s/ (Table 5.1: Columns 5 and 6). This reflects the unique characteristics of the Chinese pronunciation system, one in which words starting with fricative consonants must be followed with a vowel sound. Consequently, some of the lecturers habitually added a non-existing vowel to those English words ending with a consonant.

These data indicate that the lecturers were dependent on the relationships they could establish between English and Chinese in their pronunciation. They primarily mobilized the use of consonants and vowels between L1 and L2, making pronunciation of their first language an essential aid, not a troublesome obstacle in their EMI teaching. An advocate of monolingualism may proclaim the deficiency of these L2 pronunciations. This shows a lack of understanding concerning the realities of modern EMI teaching and learning in universities in China. The EMI lecturers are experts in their discipline but most lack intensive English training and qualifications in their own education. An alternative position is offered based on this finding, that

**Table 5.1** Phonological transfer

| Consonants: /ð/ /θ//dʒ//tr//tʃ//l/ | | Vowels: /eɪ//e//aɪ//eə//ʊ//æ//ʌ/ | | Chinese consonant-vowel combination /f//t//d//s/ | |
|---|---|---|---|---|---|
| Lecturers' pronunciation | The English words | Lecturers' pronunciation | The English words | Lecturers' pronunciation | The English words |
| [zan] | Then | [du/u] | Do | [gai/si] | Guess |
| [zi:si] | This | [tu/u] | Too | [pla/si] | Plus |
| [ze] | The | | | [i/fi] | If |
| [aze] | Other | | | [i/zi] | Is |
| [sing] | Thing | [Min] | Main | [hai/de] | Had |
| [sink] | Think | [dou/min] | Domain | [gu/de] | Good |
| [sru:] | Through | | | [an/de] | And |
| | | | | [in/ste/de] | Instead |
| | | | | [nide] | Need |
| [chuans-] | Transform | [uen] | When | [di/li/te] | Delete |
| [Chuanpu] | Trump | [en] | | [ei/te] | Eight |
| [machi] | Much | | | [ba/te] | But |
| | | | | [krei/te] | Create |
| | | | | [dao/te] | Dot |
| | | | | [gai/te] | Get |
| [an/gou] | Angle | [dang] | Done | | |
| [Jia/ste] | Just | [wai/ri/bao] | Variable | | |
| [you/ruo/li] | Usually | [pai/er] | Pair | | |
| | | [san] | Sine | | |
| | | [kou/san] | Cosine | | |

is, although Chinese and English are two distant languages (Ringbom, 2006), phonologically, these EMI lecturers' prior knowledge of their L1 did provide consistent scaffolding for L2 usage. These L1 opportunities for scaffolding were not only enacted phonologically but were also evident syntactically by the EMI lecturers.

### 5.3.2 L1 Influence on the Syntactic Structure of English

Explicit syntactical transfer was identified as another key feature in the EMI lecturers' English instruction. Often, these arbitrary rules of syntax are not commonly shared between languages and an L1 user may 'override' an L2 structure by transferring their more familiar L1 structural rule/s. The following table provides examples from the participants' EMI teaching, showing L1 sentence structure being transferred into L2, when structural rules from their L1 and L2 were mismatched.

Linguists have argued, the transfer between two distant languages, can result in the L1 having a significant role in the L2 (Ringbom, 2006). Yet others have argued the same applies for related as well as distant languages (Cummins, 2005). That is,

## 5.3 L1-Influenced English Identified in the EMI Lecturers' Teaching

bilinguals' L1 knowledge has as much influence on an L2 that is closely related or distant from the L1. This was the case for the Chinese L1 EMI lecturers in this research as the following discussion of examples in Table 5.2 indicates.

- Object-complement structure: "I don't like class quiet" is a typical Chinese sentence structure of: *subject + verb + object + complement*. The same expression in English has the structure of: *subject + verb + grammatical modifier + object* ("I don't like a quiet classroom").
- Statements without a subject: This occurs as there are no strict subject-predicate rules in Chinese sentences and a sentence can be valid without a subject.
- Statement with a question mark: question sentences in Chinese L1 are mostly statements followed by a question mark with a rising tone tagged to the end of the sentence.
- Reference to singular and plural: There is no singular and plural consistency rule in the Chinese subject and predicate relationship.
- Tense: there is no implicit grammatical mark for tense in Chinese L1. The tense of a sentence can be built into a sentence through semantics.

Bylund and Jarvis (2011) and von Stutterheim and Carroll (2006) argue that the choice of an L2 users' language structures is predictable as these structures will very likely be based on existing, familiar L1 language patterns. The Chinese EMI lecturers in this research frequently transferred linguistic structural elements from their L1 directly into their individual use of L2. A case in point is to consider how some researchers view this transfer phenomena as being erroneous resulting in

**Table 5.2** Observed explicit syntactic transfer

| | Excerpts (Sentences in brackets are adjusted for correct English usage) |
|---|---|
| Sentence structure (object-complement structure) | "I don't like class quiet". (I don't like a quiet classroom). |
| Subject-less sentence (statements without a subject) | "We need to think about why […] different view for governing the country" (We need to think about why there are different views for governing a country). |
| Question sentences (statement with a question mark) | "What it look like?" (What does it look like?) |
| | "Peers can help?" (Can peers help?) |
| | "So, anybody tell me?" (Can anyone tell me?) |
| | "We also call it what?" (What do we call it?) |
| | "When we get bigger sample, we get what?" (What do we call it if we have a bigger sample?) |
| Singular/plural form (reference to singular and plural) | "Which one is special characters?" (Which ones are special characters?) |
| Tense | "I ask you again". (I will come back and ask you about this later.) |
| | "I have tell you that …" (I have told you that…) |
| | "I don't say which test is good." (I won't say which test is good.) |

imperfect sentence structure/s. This argument only bodes credibility when the assessment is solely based in terms of the English rules, that is, when a monolingual perspective is applied. To counter, the excerpts showcased in Table 5.2 indicate that the purpose of EMI is being fulfilled. EMI classrooms in this research were not English language classes, but rather the presentation of content and knowledge via English. Therefore, the structural patterns of Chinese provided the EMI lecturers with essential support and hooks to enable them to deliver their lectures smoothly without any loss to comprehension by students. From this perspective, it is not constructive to argue that these are examples of negative transfer as they played a practical and beneficial role in this teaching and learning context. A multilingual approach would see both L1 and L2 languages being co-dependent and in a symbiotic relationship rather than separate and conflicting entities.

### 5.3.3 EMI Lecturers' Semantic Transfer

The relationship between the EMI lecturers' L1 and L2 at the semantic level was also observed. Semantic transfer between L1 and L2 includes elements such as "polysemy", and "the distinction between core and peripheral or literal and metaphoric meanings". In another words, it relates to word properties such as cognate status or "translation equivalents" (Pavlenko, 2000, pp. 1–2). As with the structural transfer discussed above, in some instances the EMI lecturer's L1 dominated the L2 resulting in unclear meaning, yet during other teaching and learning episodes, their L1 and L2 shared a semantic alignment or similarity enabling transfer to occur seamlessly and implicitly. At the crossroads between understanding and misunderstanding in semantics, the EMI lecturers were observed in their teaching using words in their L2 to create an image, rather than through their customary meaning. Examples of metaphorical or rhetorical semantic transfer are presented in Table 5.3.

The EMI lecturers were observed giving the students directions where the meaning in the L2 statement was conveyed to the students without it being linguistically correct. "Open your computer" instead of "turn on your laptop" was used by some EMI lecturers when providing instructions to the class in English. The two forms "open" and "turn on" represent two different meanings in English, whereas in Chinese "open" (dakai) is a polysemous word covering two meanings: "open" and

Table 5.3 Examples of semantic transfer

| Semantic transfer | "Now open (dakai) your computer." (Now turn on your laptop.) |
| --- | --- |
| | "Did you bring your portable computer/shouti diannao?" (Did you bring your laptop?) |
| | 'Take out your computer." (Take out your laptop.) |
| | "If the cut is not too heavy (zhong), the skin can recover itself in one week." (If the cut is not too severe…) |

"start" (or "turn on"). In a Biology class, a lecturer introduced the topic of Stem Cells using "heavy" to describe a skin cut whereas the meaning in L2 would have been "If the cut is not severe". Again, this transfer is caused by the polysemous word 'zhong'. 'Zhong' when translated into English, can mean "heavy" or "severe" but English "heavy" is not equivalent to 'severe'. For monolingual English L1 users, these would create confusion as "open" in English does not mean "start" (or "turn on") and "heavy" does not equate to "severe". However, given the context of this teaching and learning environment, where most students are Chinese L1 speakers and share similar L1 influence, this type of transfer did not create semantic confusion.

The third example was the L1 transfer of "portable computer" into L2 directly, rather than the word "laptop". Laptop is a metaphor in English – a metonymy word for "portable computer". When the Chinese L1 lecturers referred to it, they used either the non-metaphorical words "portable computer", or their own version of metonymy "shou ti diannao" ("portable electronic brain"). No Chinese lecturers were observed to have used the word "laptop" or the Chinese direct translation of "laptop". In this case, the same object was allocated different forms due to the rhetorical understanding. It may have created different images for listeners with different L1 backgrounds, but not necessarily a misunderstanding of the meaning across L1 and L2 as the metaphorical uses are related to, or a reminder of, the usual, 'normal' semantic meaning of the referent.

### 5.3.4 EMI Lecturers' Conceptual Transfer

Compared to semantic transfer, conceptual transfer goes beyond word meanings to involve cultural background experiences. Pavlenko (2000, p. 3) indicates that conceptual transfer "demonstrates cross-linguistic and cross-cultural differences". Conceptual representation can include "abstract notions" or "concrete objects". Jarvis (2016, p. 609) emphasizes conceptual transfer links to rational, intellectual experiences either "real or imagined". Odlin (2005) believes that conceptual transfer can be attributed to the linguistic relativity between two languages. However, "not all evidence of linguistic relativity constitutes direct evidence of conceptual transfer" (Jarvis, 2016, p. 616). This might indicate that conceptual transfer generates a cognitive change whereas other types of transfer appear more mechanical, affecting the bilingual speaker's language behavior but not necessarily their cognition. When observing the instructional English used by the EMI lecturers in this research, scant examples of conceptual transfer were identified, however one example of syntactic to conceptual transfer was identified. During an Environment Studies class, a lecturer introduced the history of garbage classification in China. Several times within the lecture he listed all the modifiers prior to the core word. An instance was: "In 2017, China's garbage classification system document was issued". Comparing this to the usual English expression "The document outlining the garbage classification system was issued in China in 2017", it seems to be a difference in syntactic order but in fact it reveals how "bilinguals' language backgrounds [and thinking pattern] affect the ways they prioritize path versus manner of motion" (Jarvis, 2016, p. 623). This phenomenon pertains to which information is processed or which image is visualized first, during the speaker's cognitive thinking process. Chinese people tend to start with a context such as time or location, and then move to the 'core business' for example, the issues, matters or people. With English expressions there tends to be a balance between the core and other contextual components which reflects a difference in the 'thinking/processing order' for English speakers.

A second example identified was semantic to conceptual transfer. At around 50 min into a 90-min lecture, several lecturers advised students to "Have a rest!" Expressions such as "hard topic" or "condense lesson" were also added. The image or the concept created in the lecturers' mind by 'rest' was noted to be different from the image conjured for the English expression "Have a break". By 'rest', they may have imagined and expected students literally to 'do nothing' during the 10 min between sections of the lecture. However, for English L1 users 'Have a break!' indicates the choice to have a break away from the lecture or classroom. They would imagine the students have a drink, go to the bathroom, check emails or chat to a friend. These different connotations will be dependent on an individual's prior socio-cultural experiences. The same expression may not instigate the same response in the actions of others, as imaged by the speaker. Speakers of Chinese L1 and English L1 "perceive, recognize, or evaluate the same experiences in conceptually different ways" and "have different conceptual meanings in mind when performing the same task" (Jarvis, 2016, p. 622). However, most of the students in these EMI lecturers' classes shared the same L1 and cultural background. Although no data were collected from the students, the observational data indicate that there was no perceived misunderstanding on the part of the students in relation to the lecturers' L1-influenced English expressions.

From this level of discourse there is not necessarily a clear-cut boundary between these types of transfer across languages. For example, if semantic and linguistic transfers do not generate new imaginings in a bilingual speaker's mind, then conceptual transfer does not occur. Data previously discussed in this Chapter intimated that for those Chinese EMI lecturers who instructed the students to "open the computer", those students were not imagining the literal L1 translation of 'pull it apart and see what is inside'. Instead they were able to infer the meaning as "start or turn on the computer". At a different juncture, semantic transfer is more than "a matter of naming patterns (form–meaning mapping)" or "which words correspond with which categories"; it "reflects the makeup of the mental categories themselves." (Jarvis, 2016, p. 624).

## 5.3.5 Reverse Transfer

Reverse transfer can occur at any level of communication including conceptual, semantic, and phonological. Two types of reverse transfer, syntactic and phonological, were observed in the L2 used by one of the participants in this research. This EMI lecturer was a Biochemistry Professor who had lived and taught in the U.S.A. for 10 years, and as such his English was as fluent as an English L1 speaker. Table 5.4 provides the example of the phonological reverse transfer identified during his EMI teaching.

As this EMI lecturer referred to a Biochemistry formula on the prepared PowerPoint slide, his spoken language included: "see here" followed by the Chinese "看这里". In his pronunciation, the 'kan' became /kæn/; 'zhe' became /dgə/; and the /i/ in Chinese 'li' should be heard with the tongue positioned front and middle, however in his Chinese /i/ sound, his pronunciation was closer to the English /i/. This is evidence that his tongue was slightly moved back and lower in position. Several reverse structural transfers were also observed during his teaching when he reverted to his Chinese L1 which then specifically showed an English L2 influence. The observation was that when he used two or more modifiers as attributives, he had the tendency to split them with the modified word in the middle. For example, his oral statement: 你们的竞争对手是美国的年轻人，在大学里的 whilst spoken in Chinese, followed the English structure: subject + predicate + attributive 1 + object + attributive 2 – "Your competitors are those American young people who are in universities". A typical Chinese sentence structure for this statement would be: subject + predicative + attributive 1 + attributive 2 + object – 'Your competitors are those American universities' young people': 你们的竞争对手是美国大学里的年轻人).

This finding resonates with Cenoz (2003), and Pavlenko and Jarvis's (2002) research. That is, a two-dimensional transfer between a bilingual speaker's L1 and L2 can occur within certain circumstances. Pavlenko and Jarvis's (2002) research analyzed oral narratives of a group of Russian L1 speakers with English L2. After having lived in the U.S.A. for several years, their L2 (English) started to influence their L1 (Russian) use in semantic representations and formal linguistic competence. Similarly, Cook (2003) argues that reverse transfer is likely to occur when L2 acquisition is equal to, or higher than, L1 competency, and/or there is sufficient L1/L2 proficiency to enable the transfer of learned linguistic knowledge between both languages. For the EMI lecturers in this research, all but one, did not have the L2

Table 5.4 Examples of reverse transfer

| Reverse transfer | "看这里" (from kan zhe li transfer to /kæn/, /dgə/, /iː/) |
|---|---|
| | "你们的竞争对手是美国的年轻人，在大学里的" (English structure: Your competitors are those American young people who are in universities) (Chinese structure: 你们竞争的对手是美国大学里的年轻人/your competitors are those American universities' young people). |

English competency to display reverse transfer. None had indicated an experience of having lived, worked or studied in an English-speaking country.

## 5.4 Discussion

The findings from the analysis of the observational data collected from actual EMI teaching indicate significant amounts and types of explicit transfer occurred during the EMI lectures. Two indicators were identified as influencing the L1/L2 transfer: the educational background of the EMI lecturers; and the distance between the Chinese and English languages. The EMI lecturers in this study were trained as discipline experts and received less intensive English language training in their own education. As could be expected, L1 influence then frequently appeared in the majority of these lecturers' English expressions. The particulars of the relationship between the L1 Chinese to L2 English plays the key in determining the EMI lecturers' transfer features. The examples of their explicit transfer would be different from those shown by bilinguals with genetically related L1/L2 languages, for example, German and English, and the bilinguals with genetically unrelated L1/L2 languages. Verhoeven's (1994) research identified that a strong level of explicit pronunciation or semantic transfer between languages X (L1) and Y (L2) may not be the case of languages Z (L1) and W (L2). Similarly, a moderate level of implicit lexical and morphosyntactic transfer between languages X (L1) and Y (L2) may not occur between languages Z (L1) and W(L2). Thus, it can be argued there are many Englishes in EMI depending on the lecturers' first language. Seeking 'the English' in EMI teaching is neither realistic nor feasible.

### 5.4.1 Nativeness – An Aspiration for EMI Lecturers

Chapter 7 in this book reports that the EMI lecturers in this research did not fully embrace and accept their version of English with data disclosing they aspired to an "authentic English", "colloquial English", "fluent English" and "accurate English" (Table 7.1). They described the non-nativeness of their accent and instructional language with adverse statements. Such attitudes from EMI lecturers themselves is also largely reported in the current literature (see Chap. 1). However, the observational data included in this Chapter indicate L1 and L2 transfer was the EMI lecturers' reality, with cross-language transfer occurring 'naturally' in their English instruction. For these lecturers, L1 influence is a necessary condition for their development as successful bilinguals. Cummins (2005, p. 6) argues that language transfer should be encouraged rather than impeded. The EMI lecturers either from China, Vietnam, or Finland should accept the shift towards reduced rigidity and a move away from native English norms and embrace the plurality of their English

## 5.4 Discussion

(Inbar-Lourie & Donitsa-Schmidt, 2020, p. 311; Jenkins, 2014; McCambridge & Saarinen, 2015).

This research suggests that although the EMI lecturers' L1 and English are two distant languages, they are interdependent and formed a stable construct that acted as a powerful tool in their EMI teaching. The expectation of nativeness in English does not acknowledge the reality of interdependence across the two languages (Cummins, 2005). It follows that L1 and L2 empower each other differently at various stages throughout one's bilingual development. When transfer occurred in this research, whilst the form of the L2 production may not have been perfect 'native' English, it achieved a valuable function – the 'not so perfect' English scaffolded their own English development and content delivery. There is evidence from this research to contend that the existence of reverse transfer "underscores the unstable nature of 'native-speakerness'" (Pavlenko & Jarvis, 2002, p. 219). The possibilities of reaching a very high competency level in L2 are increased if a bilingual speaker is immersed in an L2 country for a significant amount of time. However, when this does occur maintaining 'perfect' L1 for bilingual speakers is challenging, especially if competency in L2 increases to a full acquisition level. This research enables the argument that the EMI lecturers' L1 and L2 are beneficially co-dependent, and not a deficit.

EMI programs are not centered on learning English per se. Their purpose is for students to learn the discipline content knowledge, skills and understandings of their chosen field, via English (Chen et al., 2020). It is important that EMI pedagogy is considered paramount, in preference to the production of 'perfect' English exposition on the part of both teacher and student. Therefore, the relationship between EMI lecturers' L1 and L2 (Chinese and English in this context), takes on a very different persona to that of English as a Second or Foreign Language (ESL; EFL) courses and lectures. All too often a monolingual frame of reference is applied to EMI whereby the standard of English is the quintessential element of EMI success. The emerging dilemma is hence grounded in either English as 'form' or 'function' in relation to how the success of EMI teaching and learning is gauged. This Chapter contributes to the debate which challenges the over importance given to English as 'form' in much EMI research and instead argues in favor of 'function'.

An extrapolation from the findings of this research is to caution educational institutions against having assessment and evaluation criteria in EMI programs based solely on standards of authentic or native English. Policy makers as well as the EMI lecturers should be aware that extensive use of English within EMI classes is a useful and important educational strategy, but "should not be implemented in a rigid or exclusionary manner" (Cummins, 2005, p. 6), as this monolingual perspective is not supported by the cognitive reality of the bilingual lecturers' languaging processes. It is unavailing for researchers to argue that EMI lecturers' English is not authentic or lacks nativeness when there can be no single manifestation of EMI that can be applied across courses, universities or groups of students. Similarly, there is a need to acknowledge and appreciate that EMI teaching and learning does not need to mirror ESL classes as both have different purposes and outcomes.

## 5.5 Conclusion

This Chapter has reported on the analysis of the observational data of the EMI lecturers' English use from the perspective of cross-linguistic influences. Explicit linguistic transfer was identified in the lecturers' English instruction, as having been influenced considerably by their Chinese L1 phonologically, syntactically and semantically. This indicates that the EMI lecturers' English, on different occasions, was shadowed or overridden by pronunciation, sentence structure and word meanings from the Chinese language system. Based on the evidence from this research, it is posited that cross-linguistic influence is a reality in EMI teaching and should be acknowledged as such. The bilingual EMI lecturers' explicit L1/L2 transfer played a beneficial and meaningful scaffolding role in their teaching in EMI Programs.

## References

Babaii, E., & Ramazani, K. (2017). Reverse transfer: Exploring the effects of foreign language rhetorical patterns on L1 writing performance of Iranian EFL learners. *RELC Journal, 48*(3), 341–356.
Ball, P., & Linday, D. (2013). Language demands and support for English-medium instruction in tertiary education. Learning from a specific context. In A. Doiz, D. Lasagabaster, & J. Sierra (Eds.), *English-medium instruction at universities: Global challenges* (pp. 44–62). Routledge.
Bylund, E., & Jarvis, S. (2011). L2 effects on L1 event conceptualization. *Bilingualism: Language and Cognition, 14*, 47–59. https://doi.org/10.1017/S1366728910000180
Cenoz, J. (2003). The intercultural style hypothesis: L1 and L2 interaction in requesting behavior. In V. Cook (Ed.), *Effects of the second language on the first* (pp. 62–80). Mutlilingual Matters Ltd.
Chen, H., Han, J., & Wright, D. (2020). An investigation of lecturers' teaching through English medium of instruction: A case of higher education in China. *Sustainability, 12*(10), 1–16.
Cook, V. (2003). Introduction: The changing L1 in the L2 user's mind. In V. Cook (Ed.), *Effects of the second language on the first* (pp. 1–6). Multilingual Matters. https://doi.org/10.1017/cbo9780511806766.003
Costa, F., & Coleman, J. (2013). A survey of English-medium instruction in Italian higher education. *International Journal of Bilingual Education and Bilingualism, 16*(1), 3–19.
Council of Europe. (2001). *Common European framework of reference for languages (CEFR): Learning, teaching, assessment.* https://rm.coe.int/1680459f97.
Cummins, J. (2005, September 23). Teaching for cross-language transfer in dual language education: Possibilities and pitfalls. In *TESOL symposium on dual language education: Teaching and learning two languages in the EFL setting*. Bogaziçi University.
Cummins, J. (2008). Teaching for transfer: Challenging the two solitudes assumption in bilingual education. In J. Cummins & N. Hornberger (Eds.), *Encyclopedia of language and education* (Vol. 5, 2nd ed.). Springer Science/Business Media LLC.
Danish Language Council. (2012). *The status of the Danish language.* Danish Language Council.
Dearden, J. (2014). *English as a medium of instruction–a growing global phenomenon: Phase 1.* British Council.

# References

Dearden, J. (2015). *English as a medium of instruction: A growing global phenomenon.* London: British Council. https://www.britishcouncil.org/education/ihe/knowledge-centre/english-languagehigher-education/report-english-medium-instruction.

Dearden, J. (2016) English medium instruction: A growing global phenomenon. https://doi.org/10.13140/RG.2.2.12079.94888.

Gunnarsson, T., Housen, A., van de Weijer, J., & Källkvist, M. (2015). Multilingual students' self-reported use of their language repertoires when writing in English. *Apples-Journal of Applied Language Studies, 9*(1), 1–21.

Inbar-Lourie, O., & Donitsa-Schmidt, S. (2020). EMI lecturers in international universities: Is a native/non-native English-speaking background relevant? *International Journal of Bilingual Education and Bilingualism, 23*(3), 301–313. https://doi.org/10.1080/13670050.2019.1652558

Jarvis, S. (2016). Clarifying the scope of conceptual transfer. *Language Learning, 66*(3), 608–635. https://doi.org/10.1111/lang.12154

Jarvis, S., & Pavlenko, A. (2008). *Crosslinguistic influence in language and cognition.* Routledge.

Jenkins, J. (2014). *English as a Lingua Franca in the International University. The politics of academic English language policy.* Routledge. doi:https://doi.org/10.4324/9780203798157.

Jiang, L., Zhang, L., & May, S. (2019). Implementing English-medium instruction (EMI) in China: Teachers' practices and perceptions, and students' learning motivation and needs. *International Journal of Bilingual Education and Bilingualism, 22*(2), 107–119. https://doi.org/10.1080/13670050.2016.1231166

Klaassen, R., & Räsänen, A. (2006). Assessment and staff development in higher education for English-medium instruction: A question-raising. In R. Wilkinson, V. Zegers, & C. van Leeuwen (Eds.), *Bridging the assessment gap in English-medium higher education* (pp. 235–255). AKS-Verlag.

Lennon, P. (2008). Contrastive analysis, error analysis, interlanguage. In S. Gramley & V. Gramley (Eds.), *Bielefeld introduction to applied linguistics* (pp. 51–60). Aisthesis.

Lin, A., & Lo, Y. (2017). Trans/languaging and the triadic dialogue in content and language integrated learning (CLIL) classrooms. *Language and Education, 31*, 26–45.

Macaro, E., Tian, L., & Chu, L. (2020). First and second language use in English medium instruction context. *Language Teaching Research, 24*(3), 382–402.

McCambridge, L., & Saarinen, T. (2015). 'I know that the natives must suffer every now and then': Native/non-native indexing language ideologies in Finnish Higher Education. In S. Dimova, A. Hultgren, & C. Jensen (Eds.), *English-medium instruction in European higher education: English in Europe: Volume 4 Language and social life* (pp. 291–316). De Gruyter Mouton.

Odlin, T. (2005). Crosslinguistic influence and conceptual transfer: What are the concepts? *Annual Review of Applied Linguistics, 25*, 3–25. https://doi.org/10.1017/S0267190505000012

Pavlenko, A. (2000). New approaches to concepts in bilingual memory. *Bilingualism: Language and Cognition, 3*(1), 1–4.

Pavlenko, A., & Jarvis, S. (2002). Bidirectional transfer. *Applied Linguistics, 23*(2), 190–214.

Pun, J., & Macaro, E. (2019). The effect of first and second language use on question types in English medium instruction science classrooms in Hong Kong. *International Journal of Bilingual Education and Bilingualism, 22*(1), 64–77. https://doi.org/10.1080/13670050.2018.1510368

Ringbom, H. (2006). *Cross-linguistic similarity in foreign language learning.* Multilingual Matters Ltd.

Sah, P., & Li, G. (2022). Translanguaging or unequal languaging? Unfolding the plurilingual discourse of English medium instruction policy in Nepal's public schools. *International Journal of Bilingual Education and Bilingualism, 25*(6), 2075–2094.

Tai, K., & Li, W. (2021). Constructing playful talk through Translanguaging in English medium instruction mathematics classroom. *Applied Linguistics, 42*(4), 607–640.

Verhoeven, L. (1994). Transfer in bilingual development: The linguistic interdependence hypothesis revisited. *Language Learning, 44*, 381–415.

von Stutterheim, C., & Carroll, M. (2006). The impact of grammaticalised temporal categories on ultimate attainment in advanced L2-acquisition. In H. Byrnes (Ed.), *Educating for advanced foreign language capacities: Constructs, curriculum, instruction, assessment* (pp. 40–53). Georgetown University Press.

Werther, C., Denver, C., Jensen, C., & Mees, I. (2014). Using English as a medium of instruction at university level in Denmark: The lecturer's perspective. *Journal of Multilingual and Multicultural Development, 35*(5), 443–462.

**Open Access** This chapter is licensed under the terms of the Creative Commons Attribution 4.0 International License (http://creativecommons.org/licenses/by/4.0/), which permits use, sharing, adaptation, distribution and reproduction in any medium or format, as long as you give appropriate credit to the original author(s) and the source, provide a link to the Creative Commons license and indicate if changes were made.

The images or other third party material in this chapter are included in the chapter's Creative Commons license, unless indicated otherwise in a credit line to the material. If material is not included in the chapter's Creative Commons license and your intended use is not permitted by statutory regulation or exceeds the permitted use, you will need to obtain permission directly from the copyright holder.

# Chapter 6
# Pragmatic Transfer: Reflecting on the Use of EMI Lecturers' Pragmatic Markers

**Abstract** Acknowledging the critical nature of EMI lecturers as bi- or multilinguals, this Chapter continues the investigation into cross-linguistic influence now turning attention to its pragmatic features. It focuses on the Chinese lecturers' metalinguistic skills, particularly the L1 (Chinese) to L2 (English) transfer in their use of pragmatic markers (PMs). The investigation is informed by current studies arguing that highly proficient L2 language users do not necessarily make the most effective teachers, and the capacity to employ pragmatic strategies is essential to engage students' learning; and that from amongst all the competencies in which lecturers should be proficient, one of the most essential is pragmatic competence. This Chapter provides an analysis of the participating EMI lecturers' verbal characteristics of the PMs they implemented in their teaching. Whilst acknowledging individual differences, the trend of PM use and the degree of pragmatic transfer revealed in this group's EMI teaching can be explained in terms of their pedagogical ideologies and subsequent practice, culturally influenced teacher-student relationships, the EMI discipline and its relevant subject matter and the lecturers' language cognition as L2 users.

**Keywords** Pragmatic language · Pragmatic transfer · Pragmatic marker · Signalling words

## 6.1 Introduction

This Chapter reports on an inquiry into a cohort of Chinese EMI lecturers' pragmatic language use. This focus is derived from two emerging issues. Firstly, the Chinese language is pragmatically distinct from English and there is scarce research data from the literature concerning its relationship to effective teaching in the ESL/EFL area. Secondly, scholars argue that highly proficient L2 use does not necessarily make for effective teaching, whereas the capability to employ pragmatic strategies does (Ament & Parés, 2017; Björkman, 2011; House, 1996). Transposing this into the EMI context suggests successful teaching and learning could depend on or is determined by, the lecturers' language proficiency in conjunction with their ability to implement pragmatic strategies (Björkman, 2010). Pedagogically, pragmatic strategies in conjunction with the development of L2 teachers' and students' speaking fluency, can facilitate the establishment of interpersonal relationships with students and the construction of coherent discourse (Carrió-Pastor, 2020). Teachers' pragmatic competence is significant as it supports the use of effective language to communicate with greater clarity, signposts their attitudes and provides structure to their communication (Carrió-Pastor, 2020). Drawing on the data collected in this research, this Chapter looks specifically at the influence of L1 Chinese on pragmatic use in L2 in the Chinese lecturers' EMI classes.

Western philosophers distinguished the Chinese language as a different language system from Western languages such as German and English (Hegel, 1976; Jullien, 2014). For example, Jullien (2014, p. 155) asserts that in the discourse of the modern Chinese language there is a lack of "empty words" that is, functional words, to link to "full words". Pragmatic language would be under this category of "empty words". Similarly, Hegel (1976) in his book the "*Science of Logic*" made the argument that Chinese discourse lacks grammatical and functional methods, such as prepositions, articles and perhaps conjunctions compared to discourse in English or German, where such features have the advantage of producing an abundance of logical expressions. To rephrase this argument, the advantage of a logical language is demonstrated through its pragmatic strategies, that is, the use of functional words such as prepositions, articles and conjunctions.

Furthering the critique of the Chinese language, Western scholars perceive that logical and grammatical relationships within the Chinese language are predominantly indicated by word order (Zhang, 1985). This has led to the prevalent generalization that the Chinese language is yet to reach a logical stage as have the English and German languages. If these arguments, based on cross-linguistic influence theory, are taken as truisms, it could be construed that the Chinese EMI lecturers in this research would implement relatively fewer functional or pragmatic markers in their teaching through L1 Chinese, than through L2 English. With these propositions in mind, this Chapter focuses on an analysis of the PM use observed in the participant lecturers' EMI classes and three lecturers' Chinese Medium Instruction (CMI) classes. The intention was to identify if PMs were used, and if so, were there any patterns of use and what pedagogical functions pragmatic markers (PMs) enabled.

## 6.2 Research into Bilinguals' Pragmatic Transfer and Pragmatic Markers

As with the literature examining the different types of L1 influence on L2 use, pragmatic influence from L1, for several decades, has gained prominence in studies of ESL. However, research into how pragmatic strategies are implemented in EMI teaching is a more recent area of study. In general studies of pragmatic strategies implemented in ESL have mostly focused on the correlation between language proficiency and frequency use of PMs. For example, Neary-Sundquist (2014) studied Chinese and Korean ESL students in terms of their English proficiency level and their use of PMs against those of native speakers. This research concluded that those English L2 students operating at an advanced level have a broader repertoire of PM strategies in their ongoing discourse, compared to those with limited English, who had access to a narrower range of PM strategies, overusing those internalized and rarely using others; highly proficient L2 speakers used PMs more frequently and the highest proficiency students used PMs at the same rate as native speakers.

Yet other studies found there was less correlation and identified varying degrees of separation between English L2 competency and frequency of PM use, to the point where there was no correlation at all (Björkman, 2010; House, 1996). Björkman's (2010) study of spoken English in EMI classes in Swedish higher education, found that despite disfluencies and morphosyntactic non-standard speech, the lecturers were able to implement PMs to assist the students' understanding. This research suggests that the frequent use of pragmatic strategies, did not depend or correlate with speakers' proficiency in English as approximations to standard English were used to advantage.

A number of studies focused on comparing the use of pragmatic markers across L1 and L2 (Bu, 1996; Ifantidou, 2017; Kasper, 1992; Liu, 2013; Padilla Cruz, 2013). Negative outcomes for pragmatic transfer were often explained as the result of negative interference from one's L1. Liu's (2013) study reported the use of PMs between English L1 and Chinese ESL speakers. The frequency of use and the purpose for implementing the PMs were identified as major differences. It was reported that whilst Chinese ESL speakers used PMs less frequently, they often used the same PMs for different purposes (Liu, 2013). Another study examined the types of PMs being applied by ESL school students in Hong Kong and British English speakers. PMs were implemented successfully across both groups to assist with the structure of their speech and hence their interaction. However, Hong Kong learners substantially implemented referential markers with an accompanying restricted use of the conceptual, cognitive and structural categories whereas native English speakers had a wider repertoire incorporating all four PM types (Fung & Carter, 2007). In support, Vanda's (2007) research observed the language use of English L2 speakers of Chinese background and identified that this group used a narrower field of PMs compared to English L1 speakers.

Additional research was sourced which investigated the effects of PMs as a tool for improving students' learning. For example, Meyer et al. (1980) investigated if top-level structure and signalling words in texts, assisted comprehension and information recall for students. Two groups of students received the same reading – one group with PMs included and the other without. The students with the PMs in the text were more successful on comprehension and information recall, compared to the students who had no signalling within their text. Similarly, Bartlett (1978) and

McDonald (1978) also researched top-level structure and the use of PMs and concluded that both are crucial variables in learning and memory.

More recently, two studies were identified with reference to the field of EMI, specifically investigating how pragmatic markers were used as pedagogical strategies in EMI classes. Carrió-Pastor (2020, p. 137) studied and analyzed the use of pragmatic strategies in EMI teachers' subject knowledge presentations. This research found that using mitigation and boosters when explaining content knowledge was critical for teachers to motivate students and transmit the most important information. Comparably, Akbaş and Bal-Gezegin (2022) studied the pragmatic use of 'okay' in EMI teaching in Turkey. They explored its use and function by one lecturer, who was found to use this PM with high frequency during content delivery. It was noted that in this context, 'Okay' was particularly used to attract students' attention, achieve interaction, and to provide an alert prior to introducing a key point or announcing important information. These two studies have moved the exploration of PMs in EMI forward, as they approached their observation and analysis of pragmatic strategies from a pedagogical perspective. The findings are insightful for EMI lecturers in terms of improving classroom interaction and structuring the presentation of information effectively. Continuing this more recent approach to the study of PMs in EMI contexts, this research is expected to offer a contribution to the development and understanding of EMI pedagogy. The following section provides a review of the categories of pragmatic strategies and markers which have informed the data analysis in this research.

## 6.3 Functional Categorization of Pragmatic Markers

As a substitute for pragmatic strategies, pragmatic markers have been assigned to a key research area in ESL and EFL contexts, predominantly as a means to measure pragmatic transfer strategies (Björkman, 2010; Fung & Carter, 2007; Liu, 2016). PMs are "a class of items which operate outside of the structural limits of the clause" (Carter & McCarthy, 2006, p. 208), "the linguistically encoded clues which signal the speaker's potential communicative intention" (Fraser, 1996, p. 169) and "interpersonal meanings" (Carter & McCarthy, 2006, p. 208). They are "different linguistic items which have specific cohesive functions" (Ament & Parés, 2017, p. 46). If as Fraser (1996, p. 168) suggests, we encode a unit or units of text into the propositional content (or content meaning) and the non-propositional content, then the propositional content (or content meaning) would represent "a state of the world which the speaker wishes to bring to the addressee's attention" (Fraser, 1996, p. 168). The propositional content is the 'basic message' whereas what remains or "everything else" is the non-propositional segments, which are composed of signals, identified as pragmatic markers. From the relationship of PMs to the 'basic message/intent' of a unit of text, Fraser (1996) proposed four categories/clusters of

## 6.3 Functional Categorization of Pragmatic Markers

PMs. These include (1) a basic marker that reinforces the basic message; (2) a commentary marker signaling a further comment to the basic message; (3) a parallel marker signaling something complementary to the basic message, and (4) a discourse marker that signals the relationship between basic messages (Fraser, 1996). This framework allocates 'basic messages' to the center and PMs as supplementary attachments in a prescriptive and broad way, thus making an analysis of PMs quite challenging.

From a functional perspective, Ament and Parés (2017, p. 47) were able to classify PMs into four categories including cognitive, interpersonal, structural and referential. According to this framework, cognitive PMs signal the speaker's cognitive state. It directs the listener towards consideration of "how to construct their mental representation of the ongoing discourse" (Ament & Parés, 2017, p. 47). Interpersonal PMs signpost the speaker's sharing affection with, or demonstrating attitude or social response knowledge to the listener. Structural PMs have a metalanguage component indicating "the flow of discourse" to be segmented. Referential PMs signal the relationships between the utterances or between statements of ideas in the discourse (Ament & Parés, 2017, p. 47). The combination of structural and referential PMs, to some degree, align with Fraser's (1996) discourse markers. Ament and Parés (2017) distinguish a clear boundary between the structural and referential PMs. That is, the structural PMs serve macropropositional text and referential PMs serve microproposition clauses.

Meyer et al. (1980) contribute further to the discourse around the categorization of PMs by proposing the PMs relationship with the 'text'. At a top-level structure, the PMs do not function to "add new content on a topic, but give emphasis to certain aspects of the semantic content or point[s] out aspects of the structure of the content" (Meyer et al., 1980, p. 77). They further specify that PMs operate in a binary: at the macropropositional level signaling interrelated groups of sentences and paragraphs, or at the micropropositional level indicating the relationship between clauses within sentences. At either ends of this binary, the PMs are beyond the content and topic, and function as 'glue' to connect materials into various kinds of relationships. Whilst this framework acknowledges the role of PMs in organizing basic messages and information, it falls short in recognizing the potential for PMs to facilitate the organization of the speaker's mental processes and to assist in the relationship between the oral information and the listener/reader.

Considering each of the approaches of PM categorizations outlined above, a three-functions categorization of pragmatic markers is now proposed as a framework for analyzing the data collected in this research. Table 6.1 summarizes the three-functions: Cognitive, Interpersonal and Organizational including a breakdown of what each includes and excerpts from the data as examples of each category.

Adapted from Ament and Parés (2017) "Catergorisation of Pragmatic markers" and Myer (1975) "Top-level Structure".

Table 6.1 Functional categorization of pragmatic markers

| Functions | Description | Examples |
|---|---|---|
| Cognitive: Organizing the speaker's own and/or the listener's thinking | Organizing thinking | I think… Well… Eh… Like… |
| | Reformulating | I mean… |
| | Elaborating | That is… |
| | Engaging the listener's thinking | Right? Ok? You know! You see! |
| Interpersonal: Making connection with listeners | Indicating speaker's attitude and emotion | Wow! Hurrah! Yeah! |
| Organizational: Organizing the information in logical order for better understanding | Collection and continuity | Alright… Now… And… Additionally |
| | Description | For example, such as |
| | Contrast/comparison | But… However… |
| | Cause/effect | Because… So… If … then… |
| | Problematizing and solving | The problem (is…), the answer (is…) |

## 6.4 Pragmatic Strategies in the Chinese Lecturers' EMI Classes

The data collected and reported in this Chapter include all 19 participating lecturers' EMI and three lecturers' CMI teaching.[1] Observing lectures in both EMI and CMI enabled moderate comparisons to be drawn. Data reveal that across the three-functions of PMs there was an uneven distribution in the frequency with which each type of PMs was employed by the EMI lecturers. Cognitive and interpersonal PMs were rarely expressed and only by a few individual lecturers. The lack of observable PM use in these two categories may not entirely reflect the influence of L1 (Chinese), but may also mirror these lecturers' inherent less conversational and more expository lecturing styles. Organizational PMs were observed being extensively implemented, reflecting the lecturers' emphasis on managing and structuring lecture content in their EMI teaching. Organizational PMs were also observed as being implemented in the classes provided by the three lecturers who also provided CMI teaching. It is sufficient to comment that lecturers employed comparable PMs in both EMI and CMI teaching.

---

[1] Only three lecturers in this study taught EMI and CMI classes. Whilst there was a paucity of data from the CMI teaching it did provide a benchmark and insight for the examination of cross-linguistic influence on PMs.

## 6.4.1 Conceptual Cognitive Markers

The four most frequently espoused cognitive markers were "eh…", "I mean…", "I think…" and "yeah…".

"Eh" appeared as a phenomenon in a number of the lecturers' instructional language. They inserted this marker at the start and between sentences, phrases and expressions. In observing its context of use, it appeared this marker did not serve the students' learning but rather the lecturer's need. In the stimulated recall interviews after their lecture, lecturers were asked about their use of "eh" as a marker, and predominantly the reply was they did not realize they used it frequently. One lecturer recounted: "It [my speech] maybe sounds better with it. My English sounds fluent and not broken". This use of "eh" as a marker allowed this lecturer time to gather thoughts and vocabulary to continue without an awkward silence. Interestingly this lecturer did not use "eh" during CMI lectures. Another commented: "I don't even know I said that. I guess it's a habit?" This participant used "eh" consistently throughout CMI teaching, so this was clearly a speech habit and not a deliberate use of a PM to assist with language flow (Table 6.2).

"I mean", "I think" and "yeah" were used less frequently than "eh", and by fewer lecturers. The observations of their use were similar to the purpose or lack thereof for "eh". Whilst some lecturers used these PMs akin to a mantra, others seemed reliant on these PMs as 'gap fillers' to gain extra time when processing information. In this way, the cognitive markers appeared to provide psychological comfort or eased nervousness for these lecturers when organizing information in English. Interestingly, no cognitive markers in Chinese (我的意思是，我觉得，对了) were observed in the data from the CMI classes. Thus, it further confirms that the use of these particular markers is not entirely due to L1 influence.

## 6.4.2 Interpersonal Markers

Interpersonal markers were not regularly observed in the EMI lecturers' teaching. A few of the lecturers who exhibited fluent and proficient English expressions were those who articulated interpersonal PMs, such as "you see", "you know" and "Yeah? [with intonation to indicate a yes or no response was needed]", as recorded in Table 6.3.

**Table 6.2** Cognitive markers

| | |
|---|---|
| Eh, the main content in this lesson is about fine chemicals. Eh, please look at the packdge I put on your table | **Thinking process or preparing** |
| I mean… | |
| I think… I think it is about… You can call this FC. Yeah… (while she was looking at her notebook) Yeah, this kind of… | |

**Table 6.3** Interpersonal markers

| |
|---|
| You see… you see … |
| This topic is about employee career planning. You know, this topic is under the employee training and development. |
| Magic! Yeah? |
| 你看…, 你知道…, 对吧? |

An outlier was one Physics lecturer who used "you see" and "you know" so consistently and frequently at the sentence level, it became a hindrance to the flow of ideas and content for students. This appeared to be another example of 'habitual' language, rather than a dedicated attempt to engage students. Whereas PMs such as "You see" and "You know" were observed in EMI classes, their equivalents "你看", "你知道" or "是吧?" and other interpersonal PMs were not observed in CMI classes.

Although planned use of interpersonal PMs can create opportunities to maintain and reinforce positive connections with students either in L1 or L2 (Björkman, 2011), this practice was not observed in the EMI lecturers' teaching. Data from this research indicate that lecturers of Chinese background, in general, lack interpersonal connection with students whether teaching in L1 or L2.

### 6.4.3 Organizational Markers – Causation, Collection and Continuity, Description, Comparison and Problem/Solution

The EMI lecturers did employ organizational markers in their teaching albeit a narrow focus on what is possible to assist learning. Causation markers were the most frequently used of all the sub-categories of organizational markers. With the introduction of new content, rather than stipulate 'remember what I tell you', the lecturers were observed providing the reason or logic behind the content, accompanied by causation markers, for example, "Because of …", "…so…". Conditional markers were also implemented as a component of causation and included examples such as "If…, then…" when the cause-and-effect relationship between elements of the content was not strong.

Description markers were frequently used by the EMI lecturers, including "for example" and "such as", to provide additional information to a cause and effect relationship. Further, collection and continuity markers were observed to be recurring when the lecturers indicated the steps, order of processes or transitions to signify the movement or compounding structure of the content. Such PMs included time sequencing, numerals, and the parallel word "and". Observed collection and continuity markers included "Now…", "… and…" and "The next…". Noted also were the EMI lecturers' explanations to assist students with understanding similarities and differences between ideas, concepts and cases. The PMs "but", "however"

## 6.4 Pragmatic Strategies in the Chinese Lecturers' EMI Classes

and "similarly" were used to flag a positive or negative relationship. Markers of problem-and-solution relationships were only sporadically observed in the EMI lectures' linguistic repertoires compared to those discussed above. This could arguably relate to the teaching style of most of the observed lecturers who lean towards a topic-based, expository lecturing format. On the rare occasion these PMs were utilized it was in instances when a lecturer centralized a problem and then generated potential directions from which students could think about a solution. For example, "The problem is…", "The challenge is…", and "one way to sort this out…" were offered by a few EMI lecturers to assist the students' with problem solving. A summary of the observed organizational markers utilized by EMI lecturers is presented in Table 6.4.

**Table 6.4** EMI lecturers' use of organizational PMs

| Excerpts | Types of organizational PMs |
|---|---|
| Because friction causes the energy cost, so low friction is desirable. | Causation/cause and effect |
| … so this interval of convergence is $(-\infty\ \infty)$ | |
| … why? … It is because … | |
| Because of this reason, it becomes bigger and bigger … | |
| … so if we have something like this, then… | Conditional |
| … but be careful. If you want to use xxx | |
| If you didn't see the picture, come to see me after the break… | |
| If you use the macroscope to check the surface, then you will see it is very rough. | |
| If you copy 100 times, then what can you get? | |
| If we just use two variables, can you think about it? Think about only two variables. | |
| … like when you look at the … | Description |
| …such as … | |
| How should we select…? …. (Silence…) How? … (No answer). For example … | |
| ok, another example … | |
| … and let me know what is ECP… | Collection and continuity |
| … and the second point I am going to make is …. | |
| … and the next we introduce the work sample and simulations | |
| Let's choose pen size…. and turtle … pen up … and turtle go to … | |
| … ok, let us focus on this topic … | |
| … but … | Contrast and comparison |
| However, … | |
| The difficulty is … | Problem-solution |
| The problem is … | |
| A way to solve this … | |

### 6.4.4 Pragmatic Markers in EMI and CMI

Two areas of explicit L1/L2 pragmatic transfer were observed when comparing the data from the lecturers' EMI and CMI classes. Firstly, when using causation (including conditional) markers some lecturers used "because" and "so" within one utterance or sentence. An example listed above in Table 6.4 is "Because friction causes the energy cost, so low friction is desirable". A similar example was identified with the conditional markers, "if" and "then", − "If you use the macroscope to check the surface, then you will see it is very rough". Based on Chinese pragmatic rules, "Because" and "so" often appear as a pair and used within one sentence, as is, "if" and "then". However, in English discourse, this is not the case. These EMI lecturers followed the Chinese pragmatic rules when using these markers, which signified explicit pragmatic transfer in their PM use.

Secondly, in English, when students are confronting either noticeably similar or contrastingly different relationships between multiple entities, the use of contrast markers will predictably be in play. However, data in this research reveal that some EMI lecturers did not use contrast markers when comparisons could assist with student learning. For example, one lecturer in his International Relationship class compared Trump, Xi and Obama's leadership styles. His lecture was information delivery in a descriptive format moving between the three, listing a number of points for each, without any contrast markers. The details were presented in linear format where students were not engaged to think beyond the list of leadership characteristics – it was presented as a memorization exercise. In the stimulated recall interview after the lecture, he conceded: "I never thought about we should use the Markers to make things clear. The relationship is so obvious, and students can work it out." This example of omitting contrast markers is not an isolated case. Another lecturer was observed to use very few markers when analyzing the differences between two products. During his interview and when asked about the use of PMs to aid student understanding, he justified his approach as: "Do you mean the 'glue' you use to make your content stick together? You should know that Chinese people sometimes play indirect games. We call it 'dian dao wei zhi' which means 'touch it lightly' or even pause before touching it and we leave enough room for students to do a bit of the thinking job". This lecturer's comment does not only signify his approach to pragmatic transfer through PM use, but demonstrates a case of 'cultural transfer'.

### 6.5 Discussion – The Influential Factors to the Chinese Lecturers' Pragmatic Strategies

Overall, data from this research reveal three key findings in terms of the EMI lecturers' use of pragmatic strategies. Firstly, the use of cognitive markers related to the EMI lecturers' capability and proficiency in English as their second/foreign language. Secondly, interpersonal markers were observed infrequently in both EMI

## 6.5 Discussion – The Influential Factors to the Chinese Lecturers' Pragmatic Strategies

and CMI lectures across the group. From the analysis of the data, it is purported that the rare use of interpersonal markers is related to the EMI lecturers' pedagogical stance, the majority adhering to expository lecturing style, rather than a constructivist approach which would seek engagement and interaction with students. Given the mode of teaching was face-to-face lecturing, it could have been expected that interpersonal markers might have been more consistently employed as the lecturers' addressed their audience – the students. Thirdly, organizational markers were frequently and successfully implemented to signify relationships of causation, description, collection and continuity. Finally contrast and problem-solution markers were less frequently used.

The characteristics of pragmatic strategies identified in this research, do not substantiate the critique by Western scholars that there is a deficit in Chinese discourse, in terms of logical expressions, due to a lack of functional or empty words – pragmatic markers (Hegel, 1976; Jullien, 2014). This research did not examine the frequency, numerically, of the EMI lecturers' PMs in use, but it can be safely argued that they used some types of pragmatic strategies more often than the others. The EMI lecturers' use of pragmatic strategies was much more multifaceted than the linear claim made by early researchers that ESL or EFL speakers used PMs less frequently and were less aware of the multifunctional uses of PMs when compared to English native peers (Vanda, 2007; Yates, 2011). Notwithstanding some individual differences, the trend of PM use and the degree of pragmatic transfer revealed in this group's EMI teaching can be explained in terms of their pedagogical ideologies and practice, culturally influenced teacher-student relationships, the EMI subject matter, and the lecturers' language cognition as L2 users.

### 6.5.1 Pedagogical Influence

As reported in Chaps. 3 and 4, the EMI lecturers' pedagogical and instructional practices are on the continuum between expository and constructivist teaching, with a weighting across the 19 participants towards expository practice. That is, more lecturers focused on presenting knowledge, delivered via lengthy content directed oration, which resulted in the more frequent use of organizational PMs. Their instruction was observed to be topic-based rather than problem-driven, as a lock-step approach, section by section, was generally observed. Further, the lecturers' dominant expository teaching style impacted some types of pragmatic markers but not all. They demonstrated their objective to support students' learning and understanding of content knowledge through cognitive engagement, with less concern for emotional and behavioral engagement. These findings parallel the analysis of pragmatic marker use by the EMI lecturers presented in this Chapter. Less concern for engaging students emotionally explains the limited usage of interpersonal markers; the focus on direct presentation and demonstration by the lecturers explains the rich employment of markers in causation, collection and continuity and description. The use of organizational PMs afforded the students more cognitive support to process information.

## 6.5.2 Contextual Influence

In Chap. 2, a conceptualization of 'medium' (Halliday, 1999; Murray, 1988) was advanced. Accordingly, the Chinese lecturers' teaching through EMI was implemented in the same physical space as the students, involved visual and aural channels, and the mode of teaching was via an oral lecture-tutoring combination, comprising lecturing, explanation, conversation and discussion. Through this medium, the classes could have been expected to be rich, synchronous interactions. Rubin (1987) argued that applying a synchronous medium in teaching promotes an immediacy of interaction between lecturers and students both physically and psychologically. The role of pragmatic language or pragmatic markers is to tailor this mode and boost opportunities for students' participation – actions and reactions. This is especially important in EMI teaching when lecturers and students both use English as an additional language (Rubin, 1987). However, in this research the sparse use of interpersonal PMs reveals the lecturers' intentions towards establishing their position of power and authority with less regard to engaging the students emotionally. In conjunction with the EMI lecturers' pedagogical position influencing their scarce use of interpersonal PMs, the impact of tenor, which reflects the mainstream contextual situation – the institutional, social and/or cultural context – may have also influenced the Chinese EMI lecturers' use of certain PMs.

## 6.5.3 Influence from Subject Matter

Scholars assumed that a synchronous medium of instruction has the potential to lead to more engagement with students but may also be less rigorous in teaching actual content (Chafe, 1985; Rubin, 1987). The first assumption has been disaccorded with the finding as discussed above. The second claim is also disproved by the evidence of this research. The lecturers rigorously constructed and deconstructed the content with the use of organizational markers resulting in their teaching brandishing a 'bookish', 'follow the textbook' style. The influence of the field, the discipline and subject matter to be taught, could be argued as contributing to this mode. In this research it was particularly so for the STEM lecturers. The characteristics of the 'hard' subjects contributed to a more written-like mode of teaching being adopted by the EMI lecturers.

## 6.5.4 Language Influence

As reported in this research, having English as a second language is an impact factor for the observed use of pragmatic markers by the Chinese lecturers. For those with less confidence and competence, cognitive markers in their lecturing indicated their mental processing was under pressure and they needed more 'thinking time' to formulate their expressions. The PMs in this situation functioned as a strategy to disrupt 'uncomfortable' silences for the lecturers and possibly students. For others, cognitive markers demonstrated their, often unconscious, habits in their speech which offered no aid to understanding but were rather identified as a distracting feature of the lecturing style. Earlier research claimed that the frequency of PM use was influenced most significantly by the person's L2 capability (Björkman, 2010, 2011; Flowerdew, 1994; Fung & Carter, 2007; Liu, 2013, 2016; Neary-Sundquist, 2014; Vanda, 2007). However, the findings in this research support another argument. That is, different language proficiency may reduce the frequency of some PM use but tends to increase the rate of others.

## 6.6 Conclusion

This Chapter has focused on an analysis of the Chinese EMI lecturers' pragmatic strategies demonstrated in their use of pragmatic markers. The EMI lecturers' use of cognitive markers is related to their thinking and expressions in English, and/or to ease the stress derived from using English as a second language. The use of interpersonal PMs was rare both in their EMI and CMI lectures, and this reflects their less interactive teaching style and distant teacher-student relationship. The apt and frequent use of some organizational markers demonstrated the EMI lecturers' expertise and skills in presenting subject knowledge through foregrounding explicit logical relationships between ideas, concepts and formulae.

## References

Akbaş, E., & Bal-Gezegin, B. (2022). Exploring the functions of okay as a discourse marker in an English-medium instruction class. In Y. Kirkgö & A. Karakaş (Eds.), *English as the medium of instruction in Turkish higher education* (pp. 233–256). Springer.

Ament, J., & Parés, J. (2017). The acquisition of discourse markers in the English medium instruction context. In C. Pérez Vidal, S. López-Serrano, J. Ament, & D. Thomas-Wilhelm (Eds.), *Learning context effects study abroad, formal instruction and international immersion classrooms* (pp. 43–74). Language Science Press. https://doi.org/10.5281/zenodo.1300612

Bartlett, B. (1978). *Top-level structure as an organizational strategy for recall of classroom text* (Unpublished Doctoral Dissertation). Arizona State University.

Björkman, B. (2010). So you think you can ELF: English as a lingua Franca as the medium of instruction. *Hermes – Journal of Language and Communication Studies, 45*, 77–96.

Björkman, B. (2011). Pragmatic strategies in English as an academic lingua franca: Ways of achieving communicative effectiveness? *Journal of Pragmatics, 43*(4), 950–964.

Bu, J. (1996). Swedish modal particles in a contrastive perspective. *Language Sciences, 18*(1), 393–427.

Carrió-Pastor, M. (2020). English as a medium of instruction: What about pragmatic competence? In M. Carrió-Pastor (Ed.), *Internationalising learning in higher education the challenges of English as a medium of instruction* (pp. 137–153). Springer Nature.

Carter, R., & McCarthy, M. (2006). *Cambridge grammar of English: A comprehensive guide.* Cambridge University Press.

Chafe, W. (1985). Linguistic differences produced by differences between speaking and writing. In D. Olson, N.Torrance, & A. Hildyard (Eds.), *Literacy, language, and learning* (pp. 105–124). Cambridge University Press.

Flowerdew, J. (1994). Research of relevance to second language lecture comprehension: An overview. In J. Flowerdew (Ed.), *Academic listening research perspectives* (pp. 1–29). The University of Cambridge.

Fraser, B. (1996). Pragmatic markers. *International Pragmatics Association, 6*(2), 167–190.

Fung, L., & Carter, R. (2007). Discourse markers and spoken English: Native and learner use in pedagogic settings. *Applied Linguistics, 28*(3), 410–439.

Halliday, M. A. (1999). The notion of 'context' in language education. In M. Ghadessy (Ed.), *Text and context in Funcitonal linguistics* (pp. 1–24). John Benjamins. https://doi.org/10.1075/cilt.169.04hal

Hegel, G. (1976). *Science of logic* (A. V. Miller, Trans.). Routledge.

House, J. (1996). Developing pragmatic fluency in English as a foreign language. *Studies in Second Language Acquisition, 18*(2), 225–252.

Ifantidou, E. (2017). Pragmatic transfer, relevance and procedural meaning in L2. *International Review of Pragmatics, 9,* 82–133. https://doi.org/10.1163/18773109-00901003

Jullien, F. (2014). *On the universal: The uniform, the common and dialogue between cultures* (M. Richardson & K. Fijalkowski, Trans.). Polity.

Kasper, G. (1992). Pragmatic transfer. *Second Language Research, 8*(3), 203–231.

Liu, B. (2013). Effect of first language on the use of English discourse markers by 11 Chinese speakers of English. *Journal of Pragmatics, 45,* 149–172.

Liu, B. (2016). Effect of L2 exposure: From a perspective of discourse markers. *Applied Linguistics Review, 7*(1), 73–98.

McDonald, G. (1978). *The effects of instruction in the use of an abstract structural schema as an aid to comprehension and recall of written discourse* (Unpublished Doctoral Dissertation). Polytechnic Institute and State University.

Meyer, B. (1975). Identification of the structure of prose and its implications for the study of reading and memory. *Journal of Reading Behavior, 2*(1), 7–47.

Meyer, B. J., Brandt, D. M., & Bluth, G. J. (1980). Use of top-level structure in text: Key for reading comprehension of ninth-grade students. *Reading Research Quarterly,* 727–103.

Murray, D. (1988). The context of oral and written language: A framework for mode and medium switching. *Language in Society, 17,* 351–373.

Neary-Sundquist, C. (2014). The use of pragmatic markers across proficiency levels in second language speech. *Studies in Second Language Learning and Teaching, 4*(4), 637–663.

Padilla Cruz, M. (2013). Understanding and overcoming pragmatic failure in intercultural communication: From focus on speakers to focus on hearers. *IRAL, International Review of Applied Linguistics in Language Teaching, 51*(1), 23–54.

Rubin, D. L. (1987). Divergence and convergence between oral and written communication. *Topics in Language Disorders, 7*(4), 1–18. https://doi.org/10.1097/00011363-198709000-00003

Vanda, K. (2007). Native speaker and non-native speaker discourse marker use. *Argumentum, 3,* 46–53.

Yates, L. (2011). Interaction, language learning and social inclusion in early settlement. *International Journal of Bilingual Education and Bilingualism, 14*(4), 457–471.

Zhang, L. (1985, March). The Tao and the Logos: Notes on Derrida's critique of logocentrism. *Critical Inquiry, 11,* 385–398. The University of Chicago.

**Open Access** This chapter is licensed under the terms of the Creative Commons Attribution 4.0 International License (http://creativecommons.org/licenses/by/4.0/), which permits use, sharing, adaptation, distribution and reproduction in any medium or format, as long as you give appropriate credit to the original author(s) and the source, provide a link to the Creative Commons license and indicate if changes were made.

The images or other third party material in this chapter are included in the chapter's Creative Commons license, unless indicated otherwise in a credit line to the material. If material is not included in the chapter's Creative Commons license and your intended use is not permitted by statutory regulation or exceeds the permitted use, you will need to obtain permission directly from the copyright holder.

# Chapter 7
# When Structuralism and Post-structuralism Collide: EMI Lecturers' Monolingual Ideology and Translanguaging Practice

**Abstract** This Chapter activated a post-structuralist translanguaging perspective to investigate the Chinese EMI lecturers' position and practice as bilingual educators. Data reveal that there was an observed distinction between the Chinese EMI lecturers' ideology of language and pedagogical practices. In the mainstream the lecturers were not confident with their English capabilities and presented as monolingual advocates evident in their support for English imperialism. Evidence of actioning their translanguaging resources indicated a survival strategy to counter the delays in their cognitive thinking to control the language flow during their lectures. Translanguaging conflicted with their aspirations to be EMI lecturers with 'native like' English. The EMI lecturers viewed their own translanguaging behavior as exemplifying deficiencies and inaccuracies. A small group of the lecturers who were fluent in English were open and receptive to translanguaging practices. This group of lecturers, whilst in the minority, drew positively on translanguaging in their EMI teaching to enhance students' learning and engagement. They confirmed their comfort and confidence integrating both languages in EMI teaching, demonstrating a positive bilingual translanguaging identity. The argument proposed is that translanguaging as a theoretically advanced and politically correct concept is yet to be positively accepted and extensively practiced in EMI programs.

**Keywords** Language ideology · Post-structuralism · Translanguaging practice · Translanguaging identity

## 7.1 Introduction

Translanguaging is a strategy to assist with meaning making and/or articulating by consciously utilizing two (or more) languages in a bilingual or multilingual space. It "celebrates and approves flexibility in language use and the permeability of learning" by combining one's skills in more than one language (Lewis et al., 2012, p. 659). It is the reality of bilinguals (Wang, 2020) and can be used as a pedagogical resource and "a deliberate teaching strategy" (Palmer & Martínez, 2013, p. 27). "[E]ducators who understand the power of translanguaging encourage emergent bilinguals to use their home languages to think, reflect, and extend their inner speech" (Palmer & Martínez, 2013, p. 27). In multilingual and multicultural classrooms, some educators have taken the initiative to create space for their students to access multiple language resources to enhance and engage with learning (García & Kleifgen, 2010, p. 63).

Translanguaging is therefore relevant to EMI teaching as this occurs in a context where the educators and their students are bi/multilingual. However, much of the research in this field has been conducted by researchers advocating for monolingualism and consequentially identifying challenges in EMI teaching as predominantly English shortfalls. To revisit the propositions outlined in Chap. 1, a plethora of EMI research surrounds: professional learning programs conducted by English language experts and organizations (Klaassen & Räsänen, 2006; Werther et al., 2014); policies and assessment foregrounding EMI lecturers' general and/or academic English (Hsieh & Shannon, 2005); and universities' policies to promote EMI programs and English language competency as the main criteria for recruiting EMI lecturers (Costa & Coleman, 2013; Dearden, 2014; García et al., 2017; Leszny, 2007; Macaro et al., 2002; Tennyson, 2010; Werther et al., 2014). These foci across the body of EMI research is further clarified when considering the search results when 'EMI' was entered into Google Scholar in mid-2021. From within the 1.5 million hits, 2.9% foreground discussions of L1/L2 in the context of EMI programs, and only 0.4% of the articles included a perspective featuring translanguaging. This indicates that 'few' researchers consider the importance of lecturers' or students' L1 in EMI programs and even fewer acknowledge EMI teaching and learning relating to translanguaging.

This is not to say, there is no movement at all in this direction in the EMI research field. For example, recently, the translanguaging practices in several Hong Kong based high schools was studied. These included research which interrogated data relating to: Translanguaging practices to analyze how an EMI teacher created a bilingual space for co-learning in the classroom (Tai & Li, 2021a, b); multimodal conversations to explore how an EMI teacher mobilized multilingual and semiotic resources to cater for the needs of diverse student groups in science and mathematics lessons (Tai, 2022); evidence of translanguaging practices to examine a teacher's construction of a translanguaging space to incorporate the students' daily life experiences into a high school's EMI program to assist with meaning-making (Tai & Li, 2020), and the reality of translanguaging to explore the teacher's use of the iPad to extend students' semiotic and spatial repertoires for learning in an EMI class (Tai & Li, 2021a, b). These studies identified several advantages when translanguaging practices were incorporated into the EMI classes under study. These included: addressing equity issues in knowledge construction; changing the hierarchical teacher-student relationship (Tai & Li, 2021a, b, p. 241), enacting students' prior knowledge for inclusive education (Tai, 2022, p. 975); including real world learning and problem solving (Tai & Li, 2020), and creating a technology-mediated, engaging learning environment (Tai & Li, 2021a, b).

Two studies on translanguaging and EMI teaching in tertiary EMI programs were also located with findings relevant to this research. One was conducted in a Spanish university and investigated a course where students were bilingual

Basque–Spanish speakers. The course lecturer created a multilingual space during lecture time allowing students to incorporate the multiple languages available to them. This translanguaging opportunity was greeted by positive responses from the students involved (Muguruza et al., 2020). In contrast, another study conducted by a group of researchers on EMI teaching in one institution in China (Macaro et al., 2020) uncovered negligible use of L1 in the participant lecturers' EMI classes. The contention was that L2 was preferred to reinforce comprehension of the specific academic content subject knowledge in English. This finding was coupled with little evidence demonstrating the EMI lecturers' use of L1 for assisting with English proficiency, classroom management or establishing interaction with students. The student perspective was also part of this study and disclosed that they preferred English in their EMI classes with L1 intervention only when communication was dysfunctional.

The focus of this Chapter is informed by and builds on, the current literature and seeks to explore and contribute to an enrichment of pedagogical practices in EMI. It examines the EMI lecturers' language ideology and how this impacts on their translanguaging practices. Translanguaging is offered as a stand-alone Chapter in addition to, but necessarily separate from, Chap. 5 with its focus on cross-linguistic influence. Whilst the two concepts are interconnected, the distinction needs to be drawn as cross-linguistic influence is couched within a psycholinguistic perspective reflecting bi/multilinguals speakers' cognitive processes when 'doing' languaging. In contrast, translanguaging, is inherently aligned with a sociolinguistic perspective which includes political and pedagogical frames of reference beyond the realm of cross-linguistic influence. The following section reviews the epistemology of translanguaging to assist with the data analysis and generation of the findings.

## 7.2 A Post-structuralist Theorization of Translanguaging

Translanguaging although 'legitimate' can be considered an 'unconventional' meaning making system achieved through blurring the boundaries between languages, discourses and systems. It is a process in and of itself, between two languages at certain moments in time and situations. From a post-structuralist perspective, translanguaging is a powerful concept for interpreting and examining teaching and learning phenomena in bi/multilingual classes.

### 7.2.1 Going 'Between' and 'Beyond' Languages

The prefix 'trans', a variant of 'tran', from the Latin, means 'across' or 'beyond', and in relation to translanguaging has been defined as 'going between' two languages or 'going beyond" one language (Baker, 2011; García, 2009a; Li, 2011). By 'going between languages', translanguaging enables bilinguals to dismantle language boundaries and allows the permeation, integration and combination of one into the other. 'Trans-ing' can be between the linguistic forms of the languages involved such as bilingual speakers' purposeful integration of their L1 words into their L2 expressions. It can also occur between different modalities of the languages, such as 'trans-ing' from reading for comprehension in L2 to writing in L1 (García, 2009b; Li, 2011). 'Trans-ing' can also occur between non-linguistic modes. Using the New London Group's (1996) notion of multiliteracies to provide a reference point, 'trans-ing' can be initiated when bilinguals use body language from L1 into an L2 context. Translanguaging is not constrained by the demands of syntax, semantics, or pragmatics as does transfer; nor is there need for concern relating to aspects of genré and/or discourse across languages.

When considering 'trans' as referring to 'going beyond' the languages or languaging, Li (2011) proposes that translanguagers bring "their personal history, experience ... their attitude, beliefs and ideology, their cognitive and physical capacity" (Li, 2011, p. 1223) into this languaging process. Likewise, García, (2009a, p. 47) clarifies further that translanguaging "convey[s] not only linguistic knowledge, but also combined cultural knowledge that comes to bear upon language use". From these perspectives, 'going beyond' aligns with a post-structuralist view of language. Translanguaging embraces the epistemological uncertainty and relativism of post-structuralism as it recognises and equalizes resources and knowledge systems bilinguals possess or can access and imbues the validity of them as double-resourced and double-knowing agents. The 'trans-ing' of resources signifies that translanguaging can extend from the linguistic to the educational domain. It can be used to examine bilingual teachers' language in their classroom practices, the material and the funds of knowledge they employ, and the pedagogical knowledge they own or could access from multiple education systems and cultural resources.

### 7.2.2 Translanguaging as a Process

The 'languaging' within translanguaging represents actions, processes, or a collection of behaviors whereby languages, resources and knowledge systems are integrated. It is described as the 'process' of using two languages in the one space for "making meaning" and "gaining understanding" of the world (Baker, 2011, p. 288). It is the 'act' of accessing various modes of autonomous languages to enhance communication (García, 2009b, p. 140; Li, 2011, p. 1223). Translanguaging is the continuous action/process itself which operates between two or more languages. Whilst the 'trans' component has connotations similar to 'language transfer', translanguaging is less concerned with the form as transfer does, in favour of acknowledging the behavior or process itself to enhance communication and understanding. Therefore, translanguaging empowers a bi/multilingual speaker with the agency to ensure comprehension is achieved by enacting language switching, seeping, translating, meshing or other innovative and untraditional methods of languages use.

### 7.2.3 Multilingual Ideology of Translanguaging

Multilingualism confers power to translanguaging as having a legitimate base from which to justify its beliefs about language articulation, structure and use (Silverstein, 1979). These beliefs and justification are not free of social, political and cultural influences. "Particularly in the bilingual classroom, translanguaging as a concept tries to move acceptable practice away from language separation, and thus has ideological – even political – associations." (Lewis et al., 2012, p. 659). Advocates of translanguaging positively acknowledge bilingual speakers' access to the additional cognitive and language resources they hold, going beyond monolingualism and nativespeakerism (Canagarajah, 2011; Cummins, 2007; Douglas Fir Group, 2016, p. 35; Kubota, 2013; Roy & Galiev, 2011). It further acknowledges that bilinguals are not two monolinguals in the one person, that is, there should not be language separation (García, 2009a). This ideology challenges notions of a unanimous, conservative, hegemonic monolingualism purported by the 'old' structuralism school. A translanguaging ideology counters the monolinguists' belief in insulated and isolated language conduits. It welcomes bi/multilinguals' acceptance of themselves and the realities of being conversant in more than one language. This ideology ascribes bi/multilingual speakers' non-English L1 as having legitimate status (García & Li, 2014), defuncting notions of a 'deficit' when translanguaging is actioned. This ideology credits translanguagers' prior knowledge, intellectual resources and knowledge systems equally across L1 and L2 (Singh & Han, 2017).

### 7.2.4 Translanguaging as Pedagogical Practice

Pedagogy is the collection of continually adjusted practices focusing on learning and the learner's needs, in response to the negotiations between teachers, and the contexts and content required by the learning environment (Watkins & Mortimore, 1999). Thus, to appraise translanguaging as a worthwhile pedagogy, the teachers'/lecturers' specific values, the needs of their individual learners, the expectation from educational communities and broader society, and how translanguaging practice relates to the complexity of the subject content, need consideration (Lewis et al., 2012). Secondly, as translanguaging is often described as "pedagogical practice" (García, 2009a, p. 45) or "everyday bilingual practice" (Palmer & Martínez, 2013, p. 27), by implication, as a teaching pedagogy it has the potential to be purposeful daily practice providing students with a model of acceptance and legitimacy for their own translanguaging action. At the same time practice must involve "standards of excellence and obedience to rules" and "achievement." Thus, "to enter into a practice is to accept the authority of those standards" (MacIntyre cited in Pennycook, 2010, p. 24). Teachers' or lecturers' performance is judged accordingly. Translanguaging might be 'ecological' or a naturally occurring phenomenon for bilinguals (García, 2009a). It would be a little 'romantic' to believe bilinguals only need an open space from within which translanguaging practice can be created (Canagarajah, 2011). Bilingual educators who promote meaningful translanguaging practices will need to ensure they examine and establish appropriate standards and criteria for these practices and protocols. Translanguaging as pedagogical practice is not simply promoting a theory into practice application. The reverse needs to be recognized. Translanguaging should be grounded in a bilingual teachers' or lecturers' languaging resource bank, to develop a practical framework that enables answers to: "How is it that bilingual lecturers or teachers know what to do and how to implement translanguaging practices in the very specific contexts in which they teach? and What are the systematic patterns or 'laws' in bilinguals' languaging behaviors that can contribute to translanguaging pedagogy and practice?

### 7.2.5 *Translanguaging Identity*

As language is a means of creating an individual's identity, translanguaging can therefore shape a bi/multilingual speaker's translanguaging identity. That is, bilinguals should be able to assert control over their 'trans-' behavior as "personal preference" (García, 2009b, p. 48), and feel their translanguaging action is an integral part of their belonging (Noguerón-Liu & Warriner, 2014), which contributes to their identity construction (García-Mateus & Palmer, 2017; Makalela, 2015; Nguyen, 2019). Thus, for educational practitioners who value translanguaging as a pedagogy it is not only for communication purposes but more importantly demonstrates and augments their identity. The translanguaging identity intersects with, but is not equal to, their bilingual identity. Research on bilingual identity indicates that for most bilingual speakers there is a systematic shift in personality when switching language use between L1 and L2 (Dewaele & Nakano, 2013, Pavlenko, 2006, Ramirez-Esparza et al. 2006; Veltkamp et al. 2012). Findings report bilinguals felt genuine, commonsensical, emotional and thoughtful in their L1; they described feelings of not being their true selves, being less logical and less emotional when communicating in their L2 (Dewaele & Nakano, 2013; Pavlenko, 2006). In such cases the competency of the bilingual speaker across the two languages was uneven, with less proficiency in their L2. Bilingual identity can present as a combination of two conduits in the one person demonstrating an unstable self. In contrast, a positively embraced translanguaging identity enables a unified identity for a person regardless of when or how their two languages are switched, integrated, transposed, and/or translated.

## 7.3 Chinese EMI Lecturers' Language Ideology vs Translanguaging Practice

This section analyzes the views of languaging in EMI teaching held by the EMI lecturers' along with their actual languaging practices. The EMI lecturers were invited to complete a survey where one set of questions aimed at revealing the EMI lecturers' views concerning mono/bi/multilingualism. The EMI lecturers were asked to complete the following statements: (1) I am satisfied/dissatisfied with my English proficiency because … (2) I support/do not support L1 use in EMI teaching because … (3) I practice monolingual/bilingual teaching in my EMI class because… (4) I feel good/bad about my practice because …. In addition observational data were collected from the lecturers' during their teaching sessions recording the role of translanguaging in their teaching. The data were filtered by 'visible translanguaging behavior'.

### 7.3.1 EMI Lecturers' Monolingual vs Bi/Multilingual Ideology

Survey data indicate that a small number of individual lecturers were satisfied with their English proficiency. In correlation they believed implementing bi/multilingual resources was useful in EMI teaching. Among this group, some had lived in an English-speaking country for years. For them, accessing their bilingual repertoire was analogous to a linguistic liberty. In comparison, the majority of the EMI lecturers expressed a non-inclusive, hegemonic, monolingual view with the justification that English-only instruction enabled them and their students to be immersed in the language moving towards L2 language improvement. However, contradicting these answers, the survey data also captured their self-criticism of their English as being "not authentic", "with accent" and "not fluent" (Table 7.1). This finding resonates with the results of other researchers interested in EMI studies (Inbar-Lourie & Donitsa-Schmidt, 2020; Jenkins, 2018; Jiang et al., 2019; McCambridge & Saarinen, 2015; Phillipson, 2015). Accommodating the superiority of native English in favour of their own variations is rooted in these EMI lecturers' ideology. Their narratives also reflected their institution's position on and requirement for monolingual instruction. The data indicate that the proposition of English imperialism robustly influenced these lecturers' self-confidence and self-assessment. Being a bilingual seems to have kindled a sense of shame in their ability with any sense of pride as academics and educators being submerged under this view of English imperialism. These lecturers disregarded and undervalued their pedagogical experience as a teaching professional, ignored their subject knowledge and what they could offer as an academic.

The labelling of 'English' Medium Instruction is not innocent in directing some lecturers' compliance with English purism. EMI is widely understood as "teaching a subject purely in English" – this EMI criterion reflects political and economic interests (Kroskrity, 2010). As the majority of the EMI lecturers in this study

**Table 7.1** EMI lecturers' monolingual vs bi/multilingual views of their instructional languages

| Selected excerpts | Themes |
|---|---|
| I am happy with my English proficiency. I think L1 in EMI teaching is useful. | Lecturers with high English proficiency supported multilingual instruction |
| I have no English problem. I got my PhD in Germany. I don't disagree with the Chinese language playing role in EMI teaching. | |
| I have over 10 years teaching of biochemical science in the U.S. I believe we can use two languages in my teaching. Two is better than one. | |
| I am not satisfied with my English instruction. I think we should focus on developing EMI first. | Lecturers self-assessing with low English proficiency supported monolingual instruction |
| I do not have enough subject vocabulary/terminology. | |
| I am short of authentic and colloquial management language. | |
| My English is not fluent. EMI programs provide me opportunity to improve it. | |
| I admire native like English. I disagree with mixing two languages in EMI class. | |
| I am not happy with my accent. I don't think mixing English and Chinese will help my English. | |
| My English is bookish. I don't know how to make it more like oral and colloquial. | |

confirmed a belief that instruction should be delivered exclusively through English, it follows that translanguaging would be viewed as detrimental to achieving this aim. This view persisted across the survey data even though research has concluded "bilingual instruction entails no adverse effects on the development of either L1 or L2 academic abilities" (Cummins, 2005, p. 6). Politically, English imperialism may be an impact factor; culturally, this view may be connected to the ideal of attaining perfectionism in academic achievement (Castro & Rice, 2003; Chang, 1998; Sue & Okazaki, 1990). For this group of EMI lecturers, their views of translanguaging are, that its outcome produces neither flawless English nor perfect Chinese. The potential for translanguaging to contribute to effective teaching and learning was not acknowledged in their views.

### 7.3.2 EMI Lecturers' Language Identity

The data collected from the two survey items "I practice monolingual/bilingual teaching in my EMI class because…" and "I feel good/bad about this practice because …", reveal responses predominantly in two categories. A small number of participants acknowledged their translanguaging practice and expressed "feeling good"; it was "not wrong" and "no clear cut" distinction between L1 Chinese and L2 English (Table 7.2). This indicated they were comfortable and confident when

## 7.3 Chinese EMI Lecturers' Language Ideology vs Translanguaging Practice

**Table 7.2** EMI lecturers' language identity

| Excerpts | Categories |
|---|---|
| I feel good to be able to explain things using both languages and I know that helps students. | Lecturers with higher English proficiency tended to accept and practice translanguaging |
| I can speak both languages well and I use both in my teaching and I don't see it's too wrong to mix CMI (Chinese medium instruction) with EMI. | |
| The program is EMI but we are bilingual. That means we cannot be clear cut about them – when we use them. | |
| I tried to use pure English and sometimes have to borrow Chinese but often worry about students' opinion on my English proficiency. | Lecturers with lower English proficiency were reluctant to practice translanguaging |
| I have managed to teach in English so far, but my teaching is not pretty, as I can feel. I would be more stylish in Chinese. | |
| I am not very confident in my English, and I use Chinese sometimes, but I don't feel good though. It's like telling all I can't deliver the class in English. | |
| I use English only in my teaching as EMI means teaching a subject in English. To mix Chinese and English may not be what the university and students want. | |
| I am not 100% comfortable with English teaching but I signed up as an EMI lecturer so have to deliver it. | |

practicing translanguaging. This finding aligns with Dewaele and Nakano's (2013) research which reported that bilinguals with proficiency in both languages incurred less of an emotional shift when switching or mixing their languages.

The majority of the EMI lecturers indicated they would prefer to use English as the only instructional language, however they described their EMI teaching as "not pretty", "not very confident", "not comfortable", "not stylish" and some indicated the need to "borrow Chinese" in their teaching. Their responses further indicated they were struggling with English only teaching; that there was a mismatch between what they thought they should be doing, and their capacity to do so; that translanguaging countered their acceptance of themselves as successful EMI lecturers. Such self-assessments did not afford these EMI lecturers with "dignity, pride, or honor" as purported by Fearon (1999, p. 1) as should be the case for all bilinguals. In contrast, their EMI class was not a safe space to use translanguaging as their collective concern was that their students might view this as a signal of their incompetence as EMI lecturers. From their perspective, concurrent use of two languages or translanguaging did not bring them consistent confidence but rather personality and psychological awkwardness. This research does not support the argument that translanguaging necessarily and automatically creates positive translanguaging-identity or bilingual identity for the majority of EMI lecturers.

## 7.3.3 Translanguaging Practice as the Norm in EMI Teaching

Whilst the survey data captured a mainstream view across most participants that challenged bi/multilingual use as ideal practice in EMI programs, the observational data revealed that translanguaging practice was the norm in EMI lecturers' classroom teaching and served intentional and specific pedagogical purposes.

#### 7.3.3.1 Translanguaging as a Scaffolding Strategy

Data indicated the EMI lecturers used translanguaging to scaffold students' learning. These situations were most often identified when the lecturers asked the students questions and/or needed to provide an explanation, or further information, in response to an awkward silence from students. At those moments, the lecturers habitually re-orientated the students' thinking by switching to Chinese (Table 7.3).

It was observed that the translanguaging in these instances was not 'switch and move on' to new information, but rather the switch was 'dwelling on' and a partial translation of the old information, the information not being comprehended. It functioned as repetition, reiteration and cluing. It was further noted that the translation in translanguaging was not accurately word for word or translation for the sake of translation. It was used for illustration or interpretation. Thus, the translation in translanguaging functioned as a scaffolding strategy to help students' understandings or meaning making. The translation appearing in translanguaging is not simply translating the vocabulary and following the syntax as with separationist languages behavior. Translation was considered as one kind of translanguaging behavior in this context as the translation brought languages together to serve one task and to build on learning.

Table 7.3 Translanguaging as scaffolds

| | Selected excerpts | Categories |
|---|---|---|
| 1 | L: We have mentioned this in our last class. Table of coding.<br>S: (silence)<br>编码的表 | Partial translation (Emphasis) |
| 2 | L: If we just use two variables, can you think about it?<br>S: … (no response)<br>T: 想一想怎么用个变量求值 | Meaning translation (Reiteration) |
| 3 | L: How do we determine the interval of convergence for a power series?<br>S: … (silence)<br>L: 收敛区间。当时我们讲的是….谁能回忆一下? | Partial translation (Cluing) |

## 7.3 Chinese EMI Lecturers' Language Ideology vs Translanguaging Practice

### 7.3.3.2 Translanguaging for Facilitating the EMI Lecturers' Own Cognitive Process

Teaching in English created an additional cognitive load not only for students but also for the EMI lecturers. This is not unfamiliar for a teacher of ESL background in a 'normal' ESL class, where the content subject knowledge is not the primary focus. According to the observational data, most lecturers engaged both languages to assemble segments of information to ensure clear instruction and information was available to the students, in order to survive the EMI class. One kind of switch or hybrid use of English to Chinese represented an overt cognitive process when the lecturer was searching for the correct English expressions or vocabulary and was obviously struggling with this process. For example, when an English expression was absent and after initiating a pragmatic marker "eh…" there was a definite tendency for them to change the code and continue in Chinese (Table 7.4). They gave priority to English expressions rather than the content knowledge.

The survey provided additional opportunity for the EMI lecturers to clarify whether, when and why they would 'translanguage' in teaching. The answers were: "I am stuck sometimes so I rely on Chinese"; "When I messed up an explanation in English, I would change to Chinese"; "Mixing English and Chinese is not nice, but I need Chinese to help with my expression." English monolingualism, did appear to be conditioned within these EMI lecturers' ideology, however, translanguaging was observed to be their lecturing reality. They drew on their bilingual resources more or less in a spontaneous and organic mode, to ensure students' understanding. Table 7.4 below provides examples.

The observational data did not reveal the extent to which the EMI lecturers were empowered to obey or oppose the discursive rules and norms surrounding translanguaging. The translanguaging observed in the actual EMI classes appeared more as a strategy to keep the lesson flowing, rather than an EMI lecturer, as a language creator being in control of when to cross the boundaries between languages. Literature claims that the moving between or mixing languages reflects fluidity of bilinguals' thinking, and negotiation of meaning (Canagarajah, 2011; Chen et al., 2020; Douglas Fir Group, 2016; García, 2009a; Kubota, 2013). In the context of this EMI research, the translanguaging is functional in purpose as Cenoz and Gorter (2017) argued; it facilitated the maintaining of the flow of their thinking and therefore speaking. For many EMI lecturers translanguaging is the key for their own 'survival' in EMI teaching; it is not a piece of perfect artwork or a pre-planned teaching approach.

Table 7.4 Translanguaging and cognitive processing

|   | Excerpts | Cognitve purpose |
|---|---|---|
| 1 | L: How to say it… eh… 就是当这两项… | Assemble information in both languages |
| 2 | L: This is eh… 这是随意性，跟过程就没关系。 | Meaning making |

## 7.3.4 Translanguaging for Emotional Connection with Students

There was a very small group of EMI lecturers in this study, who had experienced multiple years of research and teaching in Western Anglophone countries, and they were equally capable in both languages. Whilst they no doubt had the capability to implement English as the sole language of instruction, evidence of translanguaging behaviors were observed in their teaching. These examples were not for scaffolding students' learning nor to ease the cognitive load, rather they changed the instruction from English to Chinese when they switched from the direct subject matter to an unrelated topic. This included personal stories or experiences, and 'moral' education (Table 7.5). For these bilingual lecturers who were equally fluent in both languages, the factors contributing to their use of translanguaging were found through the stimulated recall interview. One lecturer expressed: "some topics have to be done in Chinese. Like what I told them about my accident on the way to the class. It is not related to their study. It is a casual talk outside of the topic".

García (2009b) and Li (2011) both address the influence of 'mode' when defining translanguaging. Their description of 'modes' includes linguistic modes such as speaking and writing and others such as audio, visual and gestural. It could be that a person translanguaging uses L1 in writing and L2 in reading; or a bilingual integrates a particular 'body language' from one's L1 discourse in his/her L2 discourse. Translanguaging used by very competent L1 and L2 bilinguals, is not necessarily related to 'mode' but more likely to 'field'. Chapter 2 addresses the relationship between field, tenor and mode. Change to one dimension will result in a change in the other two (Murray, 1988). A mode-switch precedes an associated change in field and the speaker-audience relationship; a field-switch, for example from a formal academic to a personalized format, will impact the choice of mode. These changes inevitably impact on the tenor or the interpersonal relationship between speaker and audience. The data above reveal that when those few EMI lecturers switched from an academic topic to a personal story, the translanguaging served to establish a particular relationship with the students where recounting a personal anecdote in L1, had the potential to generate a social connection and classroom harmony. This finding is supported by research which identified interpersonal or "affiliative" use of

Table 7.5 Translanguaging as a mean of interpersonal connection

| | Selected excerpts | Emotional connection |
|---|---|---|
| 1 | L: … Today we are going to have a look at the T distribution. By the way, 进来前我几乎摔了一跤, 扭了脚。我要坐着来讲，没问题吧？ | Language switch accompanied the topic switch (from academic to casual non-academic) |
| | S: (collective): 没问题老师！ | |
| 2 | L: … Who knows the answer? …. Anyone? | |
| | S: (silence) | |
| | L: 哎!你们肩负着民族复兴的重担，你们要努力啊。 | |

translanguaging when bilinguals switched to L1 for establishing an affective and more intimate connection with students and drew on L2 for instructional purposes (Douglas Fir Group, 2016; García, 2009b; Gutierrez et al., 2001, p. 128; Jones, 2017).

## 7.4 Discussion

Scholars have been emphasizing the role of translanguaging to assist with meaning making and to provide a safe learning space in bilinguals' classrooms (Canagarajah, 2011; García, 2009a). It is acknowledged that "the planned and systematic use of two languages for teaching and learning" is valuable in ESL and EMI contexts irrespective of their distinct focus on language only learning (ESL) or academic subject knowledge and language learning (EMI) (Lewis et al., 2012, p. 643). The data in this research did indicate that this group of lecturers demonstrated translanguaging practice. They used translanguaging strategies to cognitively scaffold the development of their own teaching capabilities, their students' cognitive comprehension and to emotionally engage students. Translanguaging was not practiced randomly but was rather a considered response to the students' and the lecturers' own needs. This indicates that translanguaging, even if not systematically implemented, can be meaningful in achieving specific educational purposes.

The translanguaging practice of these EMI lecturers was only 'moderate'. This can be explained in terms of their institution's instructional policies influencing their own individual monolingualist view. This was exemplified in the data which recorded their description of the institutional demands on their EMI teaching. The EMI classes were designed to be English immersion lectures in favour of any direct planning for a bilingual mode. This finding echoes the research of Macaro et al. (2020) in which English only instruction was the preferred pedagogy. However, research conducted in Hong Kong and Spain revealed translanguaging practices were more fully embraced in their EMI programs (Muguruza et al., 2020; Tai & Li, 2020, 2021a, b) leading to the conclusion that there are different language ideologies in operation across these countries.

Scholars widely acknowledge the scope of translanguaging as a process of knowledge construction involving a range of multilingual resources including languages and cross-cultural knowledge (García, 2009a; Li, 2011). Accordingly, it could be expected that translanguaging practices of the EMI lecturers in this research, would include their language, cultural and social resources and knowledge across both English and Chinese systems – a recognition of themselves and their students as double-resourced and double-knowing agents. This confers with Cenoz and Gorter's (2020, p. 307) recent argument that pedagogical translanguaging should aim at using "the knowledge multilinguals have" from "their own linguistic and educational background". The data in this research reveals that the EMI lecturers' specific and strategic use of translanguaging resources was basic and limited to integrating English and Chinese in the form of code-switching and translation. There was little evidence indicating 'trans-ing' of resources from the two systems as carried by these two languages. Whilst the practices of these lecturers could have potentially contributed to the development of translanguaging pedagogy, rich evidence of a variety of translanguaging strategies was not apparent as the impact of the prevailing ideology constrained their motivation to accept and implement translanguaging as a valid pedagogy.

## 7.5 Conclusion

This Chapter identified and discussed the use of translanguaging in the EMI lecturers' teaching through a post-structuralist lens. The data analysis enables this Chapter to deduce three findings. Firstly, translanguaging was notably organic behavior and/or strategic action rather than any planned implementation as a preferred teaching mode. Its frequency in use was dependent on the lecturers' and students' cognitive and emotional need but was also identified as a representation of the bilingual lecturers' ideology and the impact of the institution's policy towards EMI. Secondly, translanguaging behaviors enabled three pedagogical functions to be achieved: for the EMI lecturers, it assisted in scaffolding students' comprehension; it cognitively supported them to maintain the information flow during their lectures; and positively, and emotionally facilitated their connection with their students. Thirdly, most of the EMI lecturers tended to show two distinct, paralleled identities when switching languages between L1 and L2. For those few EMI lecturers who had advanced levels in both L1 and L2, they demonstrated one unified identity, feeling confident and comfortable lecturing in L1, or in L2 as the conduit language or any variation of translanguaging between the two. For the majority of those who had uneven bilingual capabilities there was a tendency for them to demonstrate two divergent personalities specific to the language being spoken. Thus, it is important for all EMI lecturers to be supported to establish a positive translanguaging identity and this is recommended as an optimal state for bi/multilingual lecturers and their lecturing in EMI programs in higher education.

## References

Baker, C. (2011). *Foundations of bilingual education and bilingualism* (5th ed.). Multilingual Matters.

Canagarajah, S. (2011). Translanguaging in the classroom: Emerging issues for research and pedagogy. *Applied Linguistics Review, 2*, 1–28. https://doi.org/10.1515/9783110239331.1

Castro, J., & Rice, K. (2003). Perfectionism and ethnicity: Implications for depressive symptoms and self-reported academic achievement. *Cultural Diversity and Ethnic Minority Psychology, 9*(1), 64–78. https://doi.org/10.1037/1099-9809.9.1.64

Cenoz, J., & Gorter, D. (2017). Translanguaging as a pedagogical tool in multilingual education. In J. Cenoz, D. Gorter, & S. May (Eds.), *Language awareness and multilingualism. Encyclopedia of language and education* (3rd ed., pp. 309–321). Open Library, Springer.

# References

Cenoz, J., & Gorter, D. (2020). Teaching English through pedagogical translanguaging. *World Englishes, 39*, 300–311.

Chang, E. (1998). Cultural differences, perfectionism, and suicidal risk in a college population: Does social problem solving still matter? *Cognitive Therapy and Research, 22*, 237–254.

Chen, H., Han, J., & Wright, D. (2020). An investigation of lecturers' teaching through English medium of instruction—A case of higher education in China. *Sustainability, 12*(10), 4046. https://doi.org/10.3390/su12104046

Costa, F., & Coleman, J. (2013). A survey of English-medium instruction in Italian higher education. *International Journal of Bilingual Education and Bilingualism, 16*(1), 3–19.

Cummins, J. (2005). A proposal for action: Strategies for recognizing heritage language competence as a learning resource within the mainstream classroom. *Modern Language Journal, 89*(4), 585–592.

Cummins, J. (2007). Rethinking monolingual instructional strategies in multilingual classrooms. *Canadian Journal of Applied Linguistics, 10*(2), 221–240.

Dearden, J. (2014). *English as a medium of instruction—A growing global phenomenon; interim report*. University of Oxford.

Dewaele, J.-M., & Nakano, S. (2013). Multilinguals' perceptions of feeling different when switching languages. *Journal of Multilingual and Multicultural Development, 34*(2), 107–120. https://doi.org/10.1080/01434632.2012.712133

Douglas Fir Group. (2016). A transdisciplinary framework for SLA in a multilingual world. *The Modern Language Journal, 100*(Supplement, 2016), 19–47.

Fearon, J. (1999). *What is identity (As we now use the word)?* Unpublished Manuscript. Stanford University.

García, O. (2009a). *Bilingual education in the 21st century: A global perspective*. Wiley-Blackwell.

García, O. (2009b). Education, multilingualism and translanguaging in the 21st century. In A. Mohanty, M. Panda, R. Phillipson, & T. Skutnabb-Kangas (Eds.), *Multilingual education for social justice: Globalising the local* (pp. 128–145). Orient Blackswan.

García, O., & Kleifgen, J. (2010). *Educating emergent bilinguals: Policies, programs, and practices for English language learners*. Teachers College Press.

García, O., & Li, W. (2014). *Translanguaging: Language, bilingualism and education*. Palgrave Macmillan.

García, O., Johnson, S., & Seltzer, K. (2017). *The Translanguaging classroom*. Caslon.

García-Mateus, S., & Palmer, D. (2017). Translanguaging pedagogies for positive identities in two-way dual language bilingual education. *Journal of Language, Identity & Education, 16*(4), 245–255. https://doi.org/10.1080/15348458.2017.1329016

Gutiérrez, K., Baquedano-Lopéz, P., & Alvarez, H. (2001). Literacy as hybridity: Moving beyond bilingualism in urban classrooms. In M. de la Luz Reyes & J. Halcón (Eds.), *The best for our children: Critical perspectives on literacy for Latino students* (pp. 122–141). Teachers Colleague Press.

Hsieh, H., & Shannon, S. (2005). Three approaches to qualitative content analysis. *Qualitative Health Research, 15*(9), 1277–1288.

Inbar-Lourie, O., & Donitsa-Schmidt, S. (2020). EMI lecturers in international universities: Is a native/non-native English-speaking background relevant? *International Journal of Bilingual Education and Bilingualism, 23*(3), 301–313. https://doi.org/10.1080/13670050.2019.1652558

Jenkins, J. (2018). The internationalization of higher education: But what about its lingua franca? In M. Kumiko (Ed.), *English-medium instruction from an English as a Lingua Franca perspective: Exploring the higher education context* (pp. 15–31). Routledge.

Jiang, L., Zhang, L., & May, S. (2019). Implementing English-medium instruction (EMI) in China: Teachers' practices and perceptions, and students' learning motivation and needs. *International Journal of Bilingual Education and Bilingualism, 22*(2), 107–119. https://doi.org/10.1080/13670050.2016.1231166

Jones, B. (2017). Translanguaging in bilingual schools in Wales. *Journal of Language, Identity & Education, 16*(4), 199–215. https://doi.org/10.1080/15348458.2017.1328282

Klaassen, R., & Räsänen, A. (2006). Assessment and staff development in higher education for English-medium instruction: A question-raising article. In R. Wilkinson, V. Zegers, and C. van Leeuwen (Eds.), *Bridging the assessment gap in English-medium higher education. Series FLF no. 40* (pp. 235–255). AKS-Verlag Bochum.

Kroskrity, P. (2010). Language ideologies. In J. O. Ostman & J. Verschueren (Eds.), *Handbook of pragmatics* (pp. 1–24). John Benjamins.

Kubota, R. (2013). "Language is only a tool": Japanese expatriates working in China and implications for language teaching. *Multilingual Education*. https://doi.org/10.1186/2191-5059-3-4

Leszny, M. (2007). Conceptualizing translation competence. *Across Languages and Cultures, 8*, 167–194.

Lewis, G., Jones, B., & Baker, C. (2012). Translanguaging: Developing its conceptualisation and contextualisation. *Educational Research and Evaluation, 18*(7), 655–670. https://doi.org/10.1080/13803611.2012.718490

Li, W. (2011). Moment analysis and translanguaging space: Discursive construction of identities by multilingual Chinese youth in Britain. *Journal of Pragmatics, 43*(5), 1222–1235.

Macaro, E., Curle, S., Pun, J., An, J., & Dearden, J. (2002). A systematic review of English medium instruction in higher education. *Language Teaching, 51*(1), 36–76.

Macaro, E., Tian, L., & Chu, L. (2020). First and second language use in English medium instruction context. *Language Teaching Research, 24*(3), 382–402.

Makalela. (2015). Translanguaging as a vehicle for epistemic access: Cases for reading comprehension and multilingual interactions. *Per Linguam: A Journal of Language Learning, 31*(1). https://doi.org/10.5785/31-1-628

McCambridge, L., & Saarinen, T. (2015). "I know that the natives must suffer every now and then": Native/non-native indexing language ideologies in Finnish higher education. In D. Slobodanka, A. Hultgren, C. Jensen, L. McCambridge, & T. Saarinen (Eds.), *Volume 3 English-medium instruction in European higher education* (pp. 291–316). De Gruyter Mouton.

Muguruza, B., Cenoz, J., & Gorter, D. (2020). Implementing translanguaging pedagogies in an English medium instruction course. *International Journal of Multilingualism*. https://doi.org/10.1080/14790718.2020.1822848

Murray, D. (1988). The context of oral and written language: A framework for mode and medium switching. *Language in Society, 17*, 351–373.

New London Group. (1996). A pedagogy of multiliteracies: Designing social futures. *Harvard Educational Review, 66*, 60–92.

Nguyen, T. (2019). Translanguaging as trans-identity: The case of ethnic minority students in Vietnam. *Lingua, 222*, 39–52.

Noguerón-Liu, S., & Warriner, D. (2014). Heteroglossic practices in the online publishing process: Complexities in digital and geographical borderlands. In A. Blackledge & A. Creese (Eds.), *Heteroglossia as practice and pedagogy* (pp. 181–198). Springer Science+Business Media.

Palmer, D., & Martínez, R. A. (2013). Teacher agency in bilingual spaces: A fresh look at preparing teachers to educate Latina/o bilingual children. *Review of Research in Education, 37*, 269–297.

Pavlenko, A. (2006). Bilingual selves. In A. Pavlenko (Ed.), *Bilingual minds: Emotional experience, expression, and representation* (pp. 1–33). Multilingual Matters.

Pennycook, A. (2010). *Language as a local practice*. Routledge. https://doi.org/10.4324/9780203846223

Phillipson, R. (2015). English as threat or opportunity in European higher education. In D. Slobodanka, A. Hultgren, C. Jensen, L. McCambridge, & T. Saarinen (Eds.), *Volume 3 English-medium instruction in European higher education* (pp. 19–42). De Gruyter Mouton.

Ramirez-Esparza, N., Gosling, S., Benet-Martinez, V., Potter, P., & Pennebaker, J. (2006). Do bilinguals have two personalities? A special case of cultural frame switching. *Journal of Personality Research, 40*(2), 99–120.

Roy, S., & Galiev, A. (2011). Discourses on bilingualism in Canadian French immersion programs. *Canadian Modern Language Review, 67*(3), 351–376. https://doi.org/10.3138/cmlr.67.3.351

# References

Silverstein, M. (1979). Language structure and linguistic ideology. In P. Clyne, W. Hanks, & L. Carol (Eds.), *The elements: A parasession on linguistic units and levels* (pp. 191–247). Chicago Linguistic Society.

Singh, M., & Han, J. (2017). *Pedagogies for Internationalising research education: Intellectual equality, theoretic-linguistic diversity and knowledge chuàngxīn*. Springer.

Sue, S., & Okazaki, S. (1990). Asian-American educational achievements: A phenomenon in search of an explanation. *American Psychologist, 45*, 913–920.

Tai, K. (2022). Translanguaging as inclusive pedagogical practices in English-medium instruction science and mathematics classrooms for linguistically and culturally diverse students. *Research in Science Education, 52*, 975–1012.

Tai, K., & Li, W. (2020). Bringing the outside in: Connecting students' out-of-school knowledge and experience through translanguaging in Hong Kong English medium instruction mathematics classes. *System, 102364*, 1–32.

Tai, K., & Li, W. (2021a). Co-learning in Hong Kong English medium instruction mathematics secondary classrooms: A translanguaging perspective. *Language and Education, 35*(3), 241–267. https://doi.org/10.1080/09500782.2020.1837860

Tai, K., & Li, W. (2021b). The affordances of iPad for constructing a technology mediated space in Hong Kong English medium instruction secondary classrooms: A translanguaging view. *Language Teaching Research*, 1–51.

Tennyson, R. (2010). Historical reflection on learning theories and instructional design. *Contemporary Educational Technology, 1*, 1–16.

Veltkamp, G., Recio, G., Jacobs, A., & Conrad, M. (2012). Is personality modulated by language? *The International Journal of Bilingualism, 17*(4). https://doi.org/10.1177/1367006912438894

Wang, D. (2020). Studying Chinese language in higher education: The Translanguaging reality through learners' eyes. *System, 95*, 102394.

Watkins, C., & Mortimore, P. (1999). Pedagogy: What do we know? In P. Mortimore (Ed.), *Understanding pedagogy: And its impact on learning* (pp. 1–19). SAGE.

Werther, C., Denver, L., Jensen, C., & Mees, I. (2014). Using English as a medium of instruction at university level in Denmark: The lecturer's perspective. *Journal of Multilingual and Multicultural Development, 35*(5), 443–462.

**Open Access** This chapter is licensed under the terms of the Creative Commons Attribution 4.0 International License (http://creativecommons.org/licenses/by/4.0/), which permits use, sharing, adaptation, distribution and reproduction in any medium or format, as long as you give appropriate credit to the original author(s) and the source, provide a link to the Creative Commons license and indicate if changes were made.

The images or other third party material in this chapter are included in the chapter's Creative Commons license, unless indicated otherwise in a credit line to the material. If material is not included in the chapter's Creative Commons license and your intended use is not permitted by statutory regulation or exceeds the permitted use, you will need to obtain permission directly from the copyright holder.

# Chapter 8
# The Research on English Medium Instruction and a Proposed Constructivist EMI Teaching Framework

**Abstract** This chapter revisits the problems and challenges in current EMI research, reflecting on issues of theoretical scope and methodological validity. It provides a summary of the findings from this research and its implications for EMI pedagogy in higher education. This Chapter concludes by proposing a practical EMI teaching framework. Its development is based on the insights gleaned from this research and the years of my experience as an EMI facilitator for academics' professional learning in higher education settings.

**Keywords** Constructivist EMI teaching · EMI teaching and learning cycle · Translanguaging practice · Pragmatic strategies · Engagement

## 8.1 The Research

In 2013, with a colleague, I received a request through the International Office to prepare a short EMI training course for a Western Sydney partner university in Taiwan. The background to the request was that the academic staff in the partner university were required to 'switch' their teaching language from Chinese to English and our task was to prepare them for this 'switch'. It was clear that we needed to search for evidence-based research data to answer our own questions: "What does an EMI lesson 'look like' in a higher education setting and what are the existing problems?" and "How can an EMI lecturer plan and implement a successful EMI program to students in a particular educational and cultural context?" As the springboard, I read a number of reports in the EMI literature. The intention was to capitalize on current research to design a theoretically informed evidence-based EMI professional learning program.

Predominantly, the research sourced reported a host of general problems, most specifically relating to 'English', including a focus on the English language proficiency of lecturers, and/or how this became enacted as the fundamental criterion for the selection of lecturers into EMI programs. Concurrently I also identified a body of research 'about' EMI which included topics such as EMI lecturers' perceptions and beliefs about their role in EMI teaching; lecturers and students' attitudes towards EMI programs; and universities' opinions on the usefulness of EMI training. I was mystified and disappointed at the extent to which the literature engaged with 'peripheral EMI research' in company with a paucity of research tackling the major issues of EMI teaching itself. I therefore refined the literature searching to include the key words 'pedagogy', 'instruction', and 'strategies' respectively in addition to 'EMI teaching'. From the dozen articles located, yet again, 'pedagogy', 'instruction' and 'strategies' were relegated to the level of descriptive words. There was little in the way of relevant research identified addressing EMI pedagogically. Nearly a decade has since passed, and undertaking a similar search revealed some differences. Although investigating participants' opinions and their English proficiency continues to dominate the EMI research trajectory in the field there is an increasing number of studies investigating teaching strategies in actual EMI classes and professional development programs.

Returning to the anecdote of the requested EMI training program for the partner university, I continued with the project and designed what I believed would be the most relevant program for the EMI participant lecturers, based on my experience as an EFL lecturer and research experience with bilingual teachers. That is, I had a vision for the content for the EMI training program to address what EMI lecturers might need, however my intent was then redirected to foreground what the EMI lecturers themselves viewed as their needs. Subsequently, I scoped the EMI training program participants to ascertain their current EMI lecturing status – challenges and facilitators – and what they anticipated the EMI training program would afford them. Consistent replies were: Language is our key problem; we just want to know how to say things in English so colloquial English would be useful; as for teaching methods, we are already experienced lecturers and we know how to teach. Reflecting on these replies raised the question: Do they really know what they need? On further reflection and considering how these data translated into a research methodology, I was alarmed to think that research reliant on collecting only opinion from the participants as data, could result in an approach that is narrow with one dimension. This was and continues to be a core methodology in EMI studies: recording participants' views via survey and interviews and interpreting this as the state of reality. My dilemma ensued in that to prepare or deliver an EMI training program, I needed to know more about what was actually transpiring in an EMI classroom. At this point, the only information available was via the literature, which consistently reported what the lecturers, the students, and the universities had to say. Such research allocates too much power to the participants, assigning them an inordinate degree of credibility whereas researchers assign themselves to the sideline.

This inspired me to be resolute about including my own observations of the educational context, along with survey and stimulated recall data in this research. Observation is critical when data pertaining to teaching practices in specific educational and cultural contexts are to be collected. It enables a development of "a holistic understanding of the [classroom] phenomena under study that is as objective and accurate as possible" (Dewalt & Dewalt, 2002, p. 92). It allows a researcher to more fully explore "What does an EMI lesson look like in a Chinese, a Vietnamese, or a

Spanish university class?" or "How does an EMI lecturer implement an EMI teaching in a particular educational and cultural context?" It allows researchers opportunities to witness first-hand, and to document and analyze the ongoing teaching and learning behaviour and encounters of both EMI lecturers and their students. We know too little of what is happening in a Chinese EMI class, a Vietnamese EMI class, or a Spanish EMI class. This resonates with the work of Macaro (2018), which suggests observing and recording what actually happens in EMI classes is an essential step to enact trustworthy EMI research, and arguably the first step towards development of EMI pedagogy. In addition, if the researcher as observer is an 'insider' of the discourse, observation will enable the research to capture direct data which "lends credence" to the researcher's interpretations of the phenomenon and context under study (Bernard, 1994, p. 143).

Returning to the training anecdote, my experience with the first EMI training program offered to my Taiwanese colleagues, furnished me with other significant insights into EMI teaching and learning. As the program of training workshops continued the Taiwanese colleagues became more inclined to reflect on their EMI teaching contexts and were more confident to share additional information: "Our students are very quiet. They have limited English and are reluctant to talk in class". These reflections again supported their belief that the challenges in their EMI teaching, was not only their English, but their students'. They were not acknowledging the pedagogical implications of students disengaging – issues not solved by 'perfect' English. The overemphasis on 'English' capabilities as being the sole culprit in determining un/successful EMI teaching and learning, sparked my thoughts that there needed to be a wider scope based on multiple theoretical perspectives to drive EMI teaching and research. The silences surrounding theoretical perspectives particularly teaching and learning theories in EMI research negates the importance for a researcher to capitalize on EMI research from pedagogical aspect and establish 'hypotheses' that can be used to analyze the data (White & Marsh, 2006, p. 31). For example, structuralist language theories would be useful in explaining EMI lecturers' languages, and linguistic theories do not have sufficient capacity to interpret the classroom phenomena beyond language. Therefore, significant data from EMI classes would have been overlooked in any EMI research that failed to engage pedagogy and teaching and learning theories.

## 8.2 Summary of the Research

This research has now been completed and the findings are reported in this book. In brief, the Chinese lecturers did not experience a major shift to their pedagogical position in terms of conducting teaching through EMI and CMI. These lecturers' pedagogical belief was determined by their rationalization of 'best practice' and shaped by the system of the institution where they worked. It is likewise impacted by the specific features of the discipline being taught. For most EMI lecturers, the instructional language switch from L1 to L2 constrained their capability but did not change their pedagogical perception. For some lecturers, teaching through EMI decreased their authority as confident subject knowledge experts giving rise to an unstable identity.

In general, expository teaching was preferred by the majority of the lecturers whereas constructivist teaching was favoured by fewer with some leaning towards a middle ground approach – combining elements of both. However, no clear boundary between the two pedagogies was observed to be the case across each individual lecturer's teaching. Each was somewhere on the continuum between the two polar ends as was reported in Chap. 3. The pedagogy or pedagogies implemented by these lecturers was based on reasoned solutions to their specific teaching contexts and could not be attributed to mystical 'culture' as claimed in the literature. There was a shared reasoning operating across the lecturers, students and university executives that whilst learning resources were abundant, the lecturers were the most important source of knowledge for student learning. Therefore, as the source of subject knowledge, it is believed the most efficient pedagogy is through one-way expository knowledge transmission. Efficient pedagogy for them means having the knowledge conveyed and outcomes achieved in minimum time. These learning outcomes could well be questioned and very likely critiqued under Western preferred pedagogical measurement, however, this research finding provokes the thought and invites researchers and educators in higher education to consider the relationship between the suitability of expository or constructivist teaching in terms of the learner's age, that is, the adult learner.

Findings in this research also exposed the relationship between pedagogy and the discipline involved. The Chinese EMI lecturers' pedagogy, in many instances, was influenced by the nature of the subject being taught. When examining the observational data across the group, there was distinction between the pedagogy enacted in the STEM-related subjects and the social sciences. Predominantly a knowledge transmission style occurred across STEM related classes, compared to those in social sciences, however, it was not an unplanned broadcasting of knowledge. Their expository approach, whilst less favoured in Western education, was implemented with intensive and conscious cognitive engagement. Lecturers implemented a step-by-step approach to unfolding the content, leading, and scaffolding learners' cognitive thinking. Comparatively, the social sciences and their related subjects were delivered through a more liberal constructivist approach. It can be proposed that STEM and related subjects can be more challenging for learners to lead their own learning, and particularly for undergraduate students whose education is, to a certain degree, at the stage of foundational knowledge and skill acquisition.

Institutionally, the EMI lecturers' pedagogy was found to reflect the prevailing educational system and therefore sanctioned the university's current needs. The structure around teaching in the University where this research was undertaken, and probably for other universities in the country, facilitates and endorses expository approaches in practice. In this specific research context, there was no separate lecture/tutorial arrangement, which highlights an additional difference from most Western systems. There were no separate tutorials at all, as the teaching format across all subjects that I observed, was a straight 90-min of lecture time. Including

## 8.2 Summary of the Research

small group tutorials would have been a luxury when the university's expectation for lecturers was to cover a large amount of information/knowledge within the minimum teaching hours allocated. Another feature of the lectures observed was the 'normal' class size was around 60 students across faculties. The venues were lecture halls where the seating organization did not facilitate opportunities for collaborative learning to be actualized. Whilst it cannot be argued that this seating and venue arrangement was the only factor determining the lecturers' chosen pedagogy, it provided no supportive facilities for non-traditional learning environments.

The next major finding was that their pedagogy was constrained by their instructional language 'switch' from L1 to L2. Whilst this switch was not observed to impact their overall pedagogy it was the condition responsible for altering some pedagogical practices in minor ways. As this research confirms, the characteristic pedagogy for most of these EMI lecturers was a prevalence towards an expository style, accompanied by more cognitive and less emotional, managerial and behavioral engagement. Switching languages impacted the degree of interaction and engagement with students. This was particularly the circumstance for those lecturers where English proficiency was a challenge, whereby fluency issues decelerated their teaching processes. This was evident when the content displayed on PowerPoint slides was not covered during the lecture or was delivered with less explanation and examples; observed to be focusing on the 'what' rather than the 'how' and 'why'. For these lecturers their efforts were on teaching or presenting the scheduled content knowledge. Any other type of interaction could further reduce the teaching time and therefore become a burden.

Language 'switching' was observed in this research, suffice to say, the EMI lecturers' instructional language was shadowed by their L1. All the lecturers I observed in this research were influenced by their L1 at some point during their 90-min lecture. This included L1 to L2 transfer, ranging from pronunciation to the use of pragmatic strategies. Crosslinguistic influence was a 'necessary' condition for the EMI lecturers' English instruction and arguably contributes to a natural pathway towards their own development as successful bilinguals. Translanguaging practices such as code-switching and translation occurred when there was a need to scaffold their own teaching and students' learning and on occasions when socializing with students. There were a few lecturers in this study having demonstrated advanced capabilities in both languages. They enacted a positive view of multilingualism and translanguaging practice, and comfortably and confidently moved and integrated both Chinee and English in teaching. I would argue that they had developed a translanguaging identity as they reside in the space where two intertwined languages and knowledge systems contribute to their sense of self. In contrast, the majority of the group were observed to have instructional English at an unequal proficiency level to their L1. They enacted more explicit transfer and translanguaging episodes arguably as a 'survival' strategy to assist with the flow of the lectures. These lecturers evidenced a view of monolingualism, with data in this research confirming they aspired to improve their English to native-like status. They did not feel a sense of pride or dignity in their L1 influence and translanguaging was not their preferred option. This group is yet to develop and then demonstrate a bilingual or translanguaging identity.

## 8.3 A Proposed Constructivist EMI Teaching Framework

Referring back to my ongoing training work again, for over ten iterations and for a number of universities in Asia I have provided facilitation on their EMI programs. Being a teacher-researcher, I find my teaching and research go hand in hand, and it is difficult to distinguish which informed which. Based on this contention, I believe it is worth sharing a framework developed out of the insights from this research and from the years of my EMI training experience. Labeled the Constructivist EMI Teaching Framework, it provides the principles of an overarching instructional design, a five-step teaching and learning cycle, EMI teaching and learning strategies, and language skills to enact the strategies (Table 8.1). This Framework is offered with a hope that it can be a working model for consideration by other EMI training facilitators. It is not offered as an 'ideal' framework suitable for all contexts and educational systems, all disciplines and all ages and levels of students being taught through EMI. It is still being trialled as further EMI training workshops are undertaken. It is being proposed as a starting point for those who aspire to a student-centered, constructivist pedagogy when delivering courses through EMI.

The rich data from research can inform teaching, and whilst teaching is not research it can be insightful for research and the teaching of others.

Constructivist EMI teaching foregrounds the need for lecturers and teachers to establish safe learning environments and harmonious teacher-student relationships. Within this context new learning is introduced as real world problem-solving tasks, and the learning occurs through the lecturer and learners' engagements in co-construction. Further, learning activities are designed for students to work in teams and to have opportunities for the application of knowledge in real world situations. In addition, constructivist EMI teaching allows the lecturer to create opportunities for students to present what they have learned, and the lecturer ensures that students' achievements are progressively monitored. Lastly, constructivist EMI teaching emphasizes objective and outcome-oriented feedback and assessment of students' learning. There is an emphasis on continuous improvement rather than scoring and ranking.

Under constructivist instruction, the *teaching and learning cycle contains five equally important steps*. The first step is engaging the students towards being emotionally, cognitively and/or behaviorally prepared for learning. Engagement can occur throughout the teaching and learning cycle, however the introduction and conclusion of a lesson can be targeted for developing emotional engagement. Creating an harmonious learning environment, to make students feel safe, comfortable and inclusive is very important in EMI contexts where the students learn an academic subject in a second language (English). Cognitively engaging students before the new learning is also essential. It can be through linking to their prior knowledge by including brief activities such as polls, surveys, quizzes, or direct questions. The intention is to stimulate the students into active thinking in preparedness for the new knowledge.

## 8.3 A Proposed Constructivist EMI Teaching Framework

**Table 8.1** Constructivist EMI teaching framework

| EMI teaching and learning process | Teaching and learning strategies | Language skills | English Medium instruction under constructivist pedagogy |
|---|---|---|---|
| Engagement | Emotional engaging | Emotional words | Harmonious teacher-student relationship |
| | | Humorous language | Teacher's responsibility to engage students |
| | | Personal pronouns | |
| | Showing care | Varied questions (e.g. open and closed) | |
| | Inclusiveness | | |
| | Greetings/concluding | | |
| | Cognitive stimulating | | |
| | Using polls/survey, stories, quizzes, heads/tails | | |
| Knowledge building | Explaining with how and why | Pragmatic markers (for cognition) | Teacher to lead problem-based learning |
| | Demonstrating with examples | | Linking prior knowledge |
| | | Conjunctions (for the top-level structure) | Teacher to co-construct knowledge with students |
| | Scaffolding through questioning | Transitional words (e.g. signalling, signposting) | |
| | Multimedia and visual facilitation (PPT, mind map, graphic organiser) | | |
| | Deduction/induction | | |
| Knowledge transfer | Designing problem solving tasks and activities | Clear instruction with steps and action verbs | Teacher to arrange students to work in a team |
| | | Sequential words | Teacher to create opportunities for students to apply knowledge in practice and real world contexts |
| | Grouping (pair and group) and task distribution | Encouraging language | |
| | Scaffolding the activity | | |
| | Application, experiment, role play, jigsaw, debate carousal | | |
| Students' presentations | Arranging team or individual presentations | Verbal or nonverbal language to show appreciation and encouragement | Teacher to ensure students' tasks are monitored |
| | Facilitating with multimedia | | |
| | Speech, demonstration… | | |
| | Scaffolding | | |
| Assessing the learning (feedback and evaluation) | Teacher feedback and evaluation | Neutral to positive tone | Feedback and assessing for and as learning |
| | Peer feedback and evaluation | Appreciative and encouraging language | Objective- and outcome- oriented |
| | Constructive feedback | Genuine comment based on fact | Future-oriented feedback or assessing to improve learning |
| | General vs specific | | |
| Allowing bilingual/multilingual use and practicing translanguaging | | | |

*The second step of the cycle is knowledge building.* As new knowledge is presented this step has the potential to be the most challenging in the teaching and learning cycle for students' cognition. The new learning needs to be connected to prior knowledge, therefore, linking to what the students have learned or know is a priority. The knowledge building step mostly involves the lecturer's information presentation thus it is useful for lecturers to become familiar with presentation modes. For example, the presentation can be multimodal through multimedia facilitation such as videos, PowerPoint slides and/or graphic organisers. For an explanation, the procedure of 'how' and 'why' with staging language can be followed; for a demonstration, the use of examples can be considered, and to engage deductive or inductive learning processes, the lecturer may consider making full use of conjunctions to make the logical relationship explicit. When questioning is implemented to scaffold learning, lecturers may find Bloom's LOT (Lower Order Thinking) and HOT (Higher Order Thinking) (Bloom, 1984) questioning techniques beneficial. Engaging students by starting a challenging HOT question may result in students becoming discouraged particularly as they are required to respond in English.

*The third step of the cycle is knowledge transfer.* Proceeding from new knowledge acquisition, the lecturer's task is then to design activities for students to internalize the learning through applying the learned knowledge in practice and solving real world problems. The activities can be designed in various forms – in class or after class for students to complete individually or in a team. For group activities ensuring each individual student contributes to the teamwork is paramount. The activities need to be varied and chosen to best achieve the expected learning outcomes. Some possibilities are role play, jigsaw, debate carousal, application, and experiment. Instructions for students to undertake the designed activity needs to be clear with step-by-step details if the activity is complex. A blurry or brief set of instructions may lead students to a disoriented state impacting on the quality of the knowledge transfer.

*The fourth step is students' presentations.* During this stage the lecturer organizes students to 'showcase' what they have learned through team or individual presentations. The presentations can be delivered through various modes such as speeches, posters, demonstrations, or written reports of an experiment, and can be assisted by multimedia. The lecturer should stipulate the precise requirement for the presentation, scheduling and facilitating the presentations by assisting students to monitor their pacing and allocated time. Creating a psychologically safe presentation environment should also be considered when students are required to make orations in EMI contexts. For example, will the presenter be encouraged to use English-only or bilingual resources when and if necessary?

*The concluding step of the teaching and learning cycle is assessing the learning.* Informal assessment in the form of oral or written feedback is the last but an important step. Feedback helps students clarify their performance or achievement and directs their future learning. It thus should be objective- and outcome-oriented. This differs from the formal assessment at the end of a semester when grading and ranking students may be necessary for institutional requirements. For constructive feedback, the lecturer may consider focusing on the performance itself instead of judging the person, focusing on the content instead of the accuracy of their English. To improve participation of the class as a whole, during presentations, peer students can be assigned an active role to ensure the presenter and the audience are both engaged. In EMI classes, the students can be vulnerable as their presentation may be negatively impacted by their English proficiency. It is especially central that the lecturer shows encouragement and makes sure students' work will not be downgraded due to their English capabilities.

*Pragmatic language strategies and translanguaging practice* can be two tools in constructivist EMI teaching. EMI lecturers can temporarily disregard their English proficiency and accuracy issues and counter with a focus on the use of pragmatic strategies. Effective use of pragmatic markers (PMs) can ensure teaching instructions are more clear to support students' comprehension. PMs consist of various kinds of signposts such as those signalling a topic change, emphasizing or categorizing the content, and re/directing the logical relationships between the content being presented. These can be implemented to guide students to logically capture the direction, the transition, the sequence and the comparison in the instruction. This strategy has the potential to contest the limitation created by 'imperfect' English. In addition, translanguaging practice can be purposefully designed into the cycle to facilitate teaching and learning. This is especially realizable in a class where the same L1 is shared. In a post-monolingual world, languages not only cross borders and co-exist, they seep, ooze, and blend into one another through people's cognition about and presentations of knowledge. The magnitude of this concept is that it permits EMI educators, from a pedagogical perspective, to address and achieve educational equality, equity and inclusiveness, and to champion the accessibility of subject knowledge for all.

## 8.4 A Brief Epilogue

In closing, it is contended that there is a vital need for researchers to collect rich evidence-based data from 'real' EMI classes in operation, from across a variety of universities in the Expanding Circle, the Outer Circle, even the Inner Circle countries. Currently, there is an imbalance between research into EMI and research about EMI; there is an imbalance between research reliant on data grounded in opinionated problems and the research which has identified actual challenges; there is an imbalance between the quantity of research into EMI language issues and the research relating to teaching and pedagogical issues, and there is an imbalance between the generation of research knowledge derived from participants-only and that based on the co-construction of knowledge involving both participants and the researcher.

This research focused on one specific set of phenomena from one generic group of participants in one educational context and captured some of the particulars and describable features of EMI teaching in this context. It has its limitations, but the aim of this book is to disrupt the current paradigms in EMI research, to contribute to a greater understanding of EMI teaching, and to inspire new research from a more critical perspective.

## References

Bernard, H. (1994). *Research methods in anthropology: Qualitative and quantitative approaches* (2nd ed.). AltaMira Press.
Bloom, B. (1984). *Taxonomy of educational objectives, book 1: Cognitive domain.* Longman.
DeWalt, K., & DeWalt, B. (2002). *Participant observation: A guide for fieldworkers.* AltaMira.
Macaro, E. (2018). *English medium instruction: Content and language in policy and practice.* Oxford University Press.
White, M., & Marsh, E. (2006). Content analysis: A flexible methodology. *Library Trends, 55*(1), 22–45.

**Open Access** This chapter is licensed under the terms of the Creative Commons Attribution 4.0 International License (http://creativecommons.org/licenses/by/4.0/), which permits use, sharing, adaptation, distribution and reproduction in any medium or format, as long as you give appropriate credit to the original author(s) and the source, provide a link to the Creative Commons license and indicate if changes were made.

The images or other third party material in this chapter are included in the chapter's Creative Commons license, unless indicated otherwise in a credit line to the material. If material is not included in the chapter's Creative Commons license and your intended use is not permitted by statutory regulation or exceeds the permitted use, you will need to obtain permission directly from the copyright holder.

The manufacturer's authorised representative in the EU is Springer Nature Customer Service Centre GmbH, Europaplatz 3, 69115 Heidelberg, Germany. If you have any concerns regarding our products, please contact ProductSafety@springernature.com

Printed and bound by CPI Group (UK) Ltd, Croydon, CR0 4YY

27/03/2026

02079484-0002